About the Author

Laurie Dewberry has experience in communications event planning, and contributes to the magazine *Paint with Donna Dewberry,* writing a column that features products that follow a decorating theme. She is skilled in entertaining, party planning and interior decorating. Laurie and her family live in Florida.

Dedication

I dedicate this book to my loving and patient husband, Joel, and to my ever-optimistic mother-in-law, Donna. It is their faith and encouragement that gave me the courage and motivation to complete this book.

Acknowledgments

A very special thanks to Kamber Sonne for her creative suggestions and editing help. I also appreciate my sister-in-law, Carly, for helping me further develop many of my ideas. Thanks to Diane Jensen for entertaining my son during much of the writing process.

Many thanks to my editor, Christine Doyle, for her help and suggestions during the writing process. Also, thank you to Christine Polomsky, Tonia Davenport and Tim Grondin for being so accommodating during the photo shoot. And finally, thank you to the stylists and designers who worked so hard to showcase the ideas found in this book. I am so grateful to have had this opportunity to work with all of these wonderful people in creating a book that has helped me better recognize my talents and dreams for the future.

table of contents

Introduction .6

Basic Materials .8

Basic Techniques .10

Shower Themes

What Time Is It? .12

Taking the Plunge .20

Fiesta, Mi Amor .28

Sugar and Spice .38

Luxury Bridal Spa .46

Something Borrowed, Something Blue .54

Fresh Laundry .62

To Everything a Season .70

Love is in the Air .78

Paradise Luau .86

Resources .94

Index .95

introduction

A wedding shower is a very significant celebration in a woman's life and should be planned with much care and thought. Not only does the shower prepare the bride with necessary items for her new home, it is a time for friends and family to express their love and support for the bride as she takes this momentous step in her life.

In creating this book, my goal was to plan both traditional and unique shower themes that appeal to a wide variety of individual tastes. As someone who enjoys entertaining, I love carrying out a party theme to its fullest potential, and I believe it's the small details that make the biggest difference.

Each of the ten themes found in the chapters ahead includes all of the details you will need for planning the ultimate shower. Everything from the invitation and decorations to the entertainment and gift-giving ideas has been provided to make the planning of your shower go as smoothly as possible.

As you choose a shower theme, consider the personalities of the bride and groom as well as their individual gift needs. If the bride is having more than one shower, or if the couple has already lived together for some time, a couple's shower or a shower with a more tailored gift-giving theme may be the best party option. Keep in mind, too, what kind of shower you feel you can make the most successful based on your time, budget or other limitations.

As you begin planning this special event, here are some hostess tips to get you started on the right track:

- Give yourself plenty of time to plan and prepare for the shower, at least a month or two before the wedding.
- Encourage the bride- and groom-to-be to register for gifts before the shower to help your guests know what the couple needs.
- When preparing the guest list, ask the bride and groom whom they would like to attend. Make sure your other guests know at least one other person so they feel comfortable during the shower.
- Select a date and time that is convenient for the bride and the guests. Weekends typically work the best.
- In choosing a location for the shower, make sure it will accommodate the needs of the party. Does it have enough space? Is it easily accessible for your guests? Does it match the theme of the party?
- Make sure you have plenty of seating and table space set up to accommodate your guests comfortably and arrange it in a way that will encourage lively conversation among your guests.
- Prepare as much of the food ahead of time as possible.
- Assist the bride with her thank-you cards by addressing the envelopes for her and by keeping a list of what each guest gives the bride.

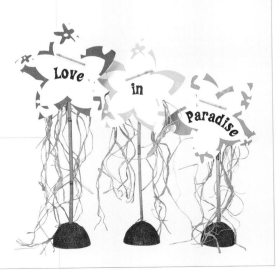

Being the hostess for the exciting event gives you the opportunity to not only honor the bride and groom, but to make your guests feel special as well. No matter which shower theme you choose, each one promises to be a fun celebration for all who attend.

basic materials

To make the invitations and many of the favors and decorations in this book, you'll need a few basic craft supplies on hand. All of these products are available at either art and craft stores, scrapbook stores or rubber stamping stores. If you can't find something at a local store, contact the manufacturer (listed in the Resources, page 94); they should be able to help you find a retailer near you.

PAPER

The paper you choose for your shower projects can function as an integral part of your design or simply as a foundation on which you build your design. Base your selection of paper on what will work best for your project.

Card or cover stock: Cardstock, often referred to as cover stock, is a heavier-weight paper. It is available in many colors, patterns, textures and finishes, ranging from smooth to heavily textured and matte to glossy. Cardstock works well as a base for an invitation.

Text paper: Text-weight paper is a medium-weight paper. It is available in many colors, patterns, textures and finishes. Scrapbook paper offers an amazing array of choices in this type of paper. Computer paper is also text-weight. Because text-weight paper is less substantial than cardstock, it works well layered onto a piece of cardstock for invitations and decorations.

Translucent paper: Translucent paper, often called vellum, is characterized by its see-through quality. It can be found in many colors and designs and is available in both text-weight and cardstock weight. Text-weight vellum works well as an overlay on patterned papers. You can print text on a piece of vellum and then secure it on top of cardstock. Any pattern or design on the cardstock would be visible, though muted, through the vellum.

CUTTING TOOLS

To help the creation of your papercrafts go smoothly, keep sharp, quality cutting tools available. You may need a few different tools to make quick work of the cutting. Following are a few you may want to have on hand.

Hand-held scissors: A large pair is useful for cutting down large sheets of paper, while a small pair of craft scissors is good for cutting out small pieces and images and for cutting embellishments, like ribbon. For quick and precise cutting of small pieces of paper, move the paper and keep the scissors stationary as you cut.

Craft knife, metal ruler and self-healing cutting mat: A scalpel-type craft knife with a replaceable pointed blade is essential. It is an all-purpose knife for cutting all types of papers. Scissors don't give you the straight, sharp edges you get with a craft knife. Keep a supply of additional blades on hand to ensure you'll always have a sharp cutting edge. To protect your work surface, use a self-healing cutting mat when using a craft knife. A metal ruler with cork backing works well as a nonslip guide for your straight cuts.

FOLDING TOOLS

One key to well-made papercrafts is crisp, straight folds. The easiest way to get a crisp fold is to score the paper first. A score is a halfcut that breaks through (or condenses) the top fibers of the paper, and it is made on what will be the outside of the fold. Following are a number of tools you may use to create a score. For step-by-step instructions for scoring and folding, see page 10.

Bone folder: This flat piece of smooth bone is usually rounded at one end and pointed at the other. For each fold, draw the bone folder along a ruler edge toward you, pressing down to score a fold line.

Stylus: You can also use a pressure embossing stylus rather than the bone folder. Run the stylus along the edge of a ruler on a slightly padded surface, such as a cutting mat, to score the paper.

ADHESIVES

There are many kinds of glues to use for different craft projects. When selecting a glue to use, take into consideration the glue's tackiness, permanence and whether it dries clearly or not. Here is a list of glue choices and the types of projects for which they are most appropriate.

Glue stick: This handy glue is suitable for gluing papers together because it is easy to use, dries clearly and is acid free.

Craft glue: Appropriate for use with most projects, craft glue gives a stronger bond than regular household glue or glue stick. Apply craft glue with a paintbrush for large areas of coverage, or with a toothpick for smaller areas.

Hot glue: This strong glue is great for using with floral crafts, wood projects or other multi-dimensional items. Keep the hot glue gun and plenty of refill glue sticks handy for touch-up jobs as well.

Spray adhesive: Stronger and more permanent than other paper glues, spray adhesive works well on papercrafts when a large, flat surface area needs to be covered with glue and you don't want the paper to shift during gluing.

Découpage medium: This spreadable glue is used to glue paper to wood or papier mâché surfaces. It also works well anytime you want to glue thin paper, such as tissue paper, to a surface because it spreads more easily than craft glue and covers a larger area more easily than a glue stick.

EMBELLISHMENTS

Ribbon, silk flowers, eyelets and charms are just a few of the wonderful embellishments that can make your invitations and decorations truly unique.

Some, like charms, are simply decorative. You can string them onto ribbon to attach them to your crafts, or you can glue them in place with craft glue.

Other embellishments, like ribbon and eyelets, are not only beautiful but can be functional too. Instead of gluing two layers of paper together, try securing them with eyelets. Close a party favor with a clip or wrap it with ribbon. Gather different embellishments and play with them to see what works best for your projects.

▼ *Clockwise from top left: decorative papers; découpage medium; glue stick; craft glue; hot glue gun; metal ruler; hot glue sticks; hand-held scissors; craft knife; bone folder; decorative ribbon; self-healing cutting mat; assorted tags and beads, charms and eyelets*

basic techniques

Making the invitations, favors and decorations for the wedding shower is easy once you've learned these few basic techniques.

SCORING AND FOLDING PAPER

Scoring a piece of paper before folding it will give a crisp fold and a professional-looking result. Scoring is especially helpful with heavy-weight papers, such as cardstock. Here I am using a bone folder, but a stylus may be used as well.

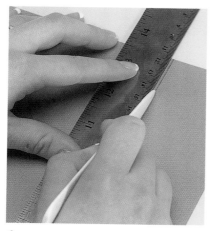

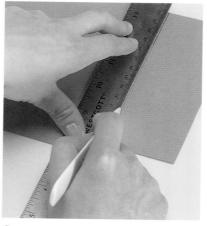

1. Align Bone Folder Along the Mark
When scoring a straight line at a marked measurement, be sure to place the bone folder on the mark, and the ruler next to the bone folder.

2. Drag the Bone Folder Down
With the ruler as a guide, pull the bone folder toward you, applying even pressure.

3. Crease Along the Fold
Fold along the scored line and flatten the crease with the bone folder.

PUNCHING HOLES

This book uses two methods for making a hole in a piece of paper. One method uses a steel die and a hammer; the other uses a hand-held punch.

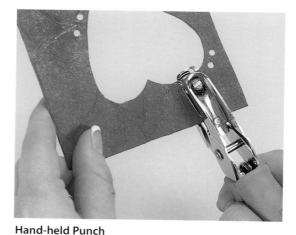

Die Punch
This is used to go through multiple layers, or where a hand-held punch won't reach. On a protective surface, center the punch where you wish to make a hole and tap several times with a hammer until you have punched completely through the surface. These punches often come in a kit with various sizes.

Hand-held Punch
This type of punch requires no protective surface. Center the punch shaft over where you want a hole and squeeze. This is often the quickest and easiest way to make a hole, if the punch will reach.

SETTING GROMMETS

Adding a grommet to your project is a quick way to reinforce a hole that is punched in either paper or fabric. A special tool is used to punch the hole and set the grommet.

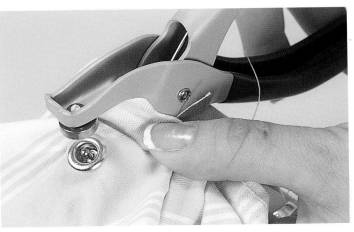

1. Make a Hole

Using the grommet setting tool, make a hole at your desired mark by squeezing the handles together.

2. Set the Grommet

Push the top grommet piece (the one with the longer shaft) through the hole. Place the back of the grommet on the shaft of the grommet setting tool and close over the top piece of the grommet by squeezing the tool handles together.

SETTING EYELETS

Eyelets really spice up the look of any papercraft project, and they are so easy to set. They are functional for holding together layers of paper, or for acting as a hole reinforcer.

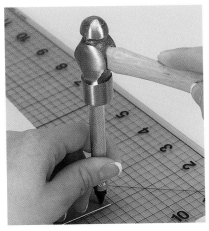

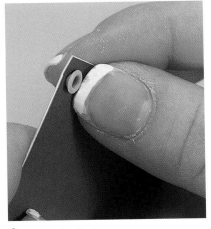

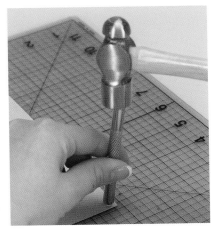

1. Punch a Hole

Punch a hole that is appropriate for the size eyelet you are using. Punch through all the layers to be held together at the same time.

2. Insert the Eyelet

Set the shaft of the eyelet through the hole, from the front to the back.

3. Set the Eyelet

Turn the piece over onto a protective surface, and using the eyelet setting tool and small hammer, spread the shaft apart to set. Remove the setting tool, and tap the opened eyelet with the hammer again to flatten completely.

Tip

If you don't want to see the back side of the eyelet, just set the eyelet through the top layer and glue the paper onto a second layer.

What Time Is It?

Time is of the essence for this bright and funky shower.
The clock invitations set the stage and assign guests one of four "time" categories around which to theme their gift: time to clean and organize, time to cook, time to play, and time to relax and go to bed. The orange, fuchsia and red in the invitation is carried through to the decorations and party favors, making this theme perfect for the bride with a vivacious personality and unique style. Now it's time for you to start planning a terrific shower!

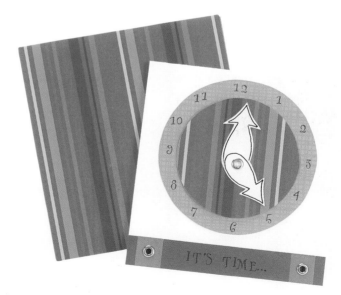

time of day invitation

Everyone will know that time is the theme of this shower when they receive this fun and colorful invitation. Use the clock face and hands to display the time the shower will be held (and restate it inside the invitation just to be clear). The bold colors of the papers will signal to your guests that the shower will be unique and festive.

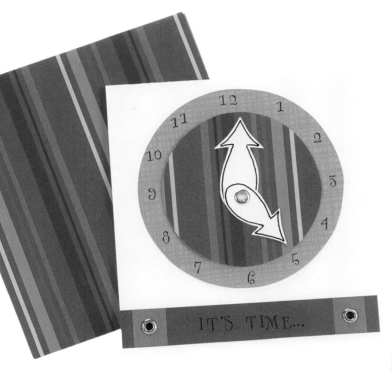

MATERIALS

8½" x 11" (22cm x 28cm) white cardstock

12" x 12" (30cm x 30cm) orange and red striped paper, 2 sheets (KI Memories)

12" x 12" (30cm × 30cm) orange linen paper (KI Memories)

purple, red and fuchsia scraps of paper

uppercase alphabet stamps (Hero Arts)

lowercase alphabet stamps (Hero Arts)

number stamps

three ¼" (6mm) silver eyelets

black inkpad

fuchsia ink gel pen

black ink gel pen

bone folder

pencil

glue stick

scissors

compass or circle cutter

¼" (6mm) hole punch

eyelet setter, hammer and mat

envelope pattern, page 19

clock hands pattern, page 19

Gift Ideas

Inside each invitation, assign the guest to one of the following four time categories: "It's time to clean and organize," "It's time to cook," "It's time to play," or "It's time to relax and go to bed." Explain to your guests that each gift should coincide with the designated time of the day.

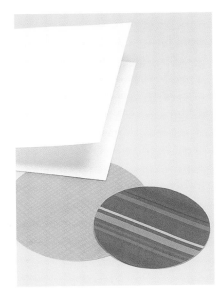

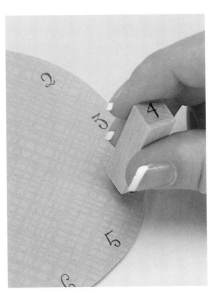

1. Prepare Pieces

Cut a 5" × 11" (13cm × 28cm) piece of white cardstock, score and fold in half. Using a compass, cut a 3⅛" (8cm) circle out of the striped paper. Cut a 4" (10cm) circle out of the orange paper.

2. Make Marks for the Numbers

With a pencil, lightly mark where you want the numbers to be stamped along the outer edge of the orange circle. Place the smaller circle in the center for placement.

3. Stamp the Numbers

Using the black ink and the number stamps, stamp the numbers on the larger orange circle. Begin with the 12 and the 6; then add the 9 and the 3. Fill in the remaining numbers.

4. Assemble the Clock

Cut out large and small clock hands using the pattern on page 19, and outline with black pen. Set the hands onto the striped circle on top of the stamped circle and position them at the time the party will begin. Punch a ¼" (6mm) hole in the center and set an eyelet in the hole. Cut a 5" × ¾" (13cm × 2cm) rectangle out of purple scrap paper and stamp "It's time..." in the center of the rectangle. Cut two small fuchsia rectangles and place on either end of the purple rectangle. Mount the three pieces to the white cardstock with silver eyelets, ¼" (6mm) from the bottom.

5. Create the Inside Wording

Cut a 4½" × 5" (11cm × 13cm) rectangle out of the orange paper. Cut four small rectangles out of red scrap paper. With the uppercase letter stamps, create the phrase "...to shower (Bride's name) with gifts" at the top of the orange rectangle. With the lowercase stamp set, stamp "date," "time," "place" and "r.s.v.p." in the center of the invitation. Glue the orange rectangle in the center of the inside of the invitation. Glue the four red rectangles in the corners of the orange rectangle. With a purple or pink pen, write in the remaining shower information.

6. Create the Envelope

Using the envelope pattern on page 19, create an envelope out of the striped paper. Fold along the lines shown. Run a glue stick along the flaps and fold up the back.

decorations

The bright, bold colors used in this shower will reflect the bride's unique style and creative personality. As you plan your decorations, consider the following suggestions.

- Place arrangements of bright orange, fuchsia or red artificial gerbera daisies in clear vases filled with red, orange and pink jelly beans.
- Set out "take-out" lunch bags on serving table *(see project below)*.
- Use bright orange, red or fuchsia tablecloths on the serving and gift tables.

- Hang a paper banner of the bride's and groom's names *(see project below)*.
- Place party favor tins in a small party tub by the front door or other visible spot *(see project, page 19)*.

bride and groom name banner *Honor the happy couple with this bright and festive banner. Hang it above the serving area or in another prominent spot.*

Cut 4½" (11cm) circles for each letter of the bride's and groom's names from a paper that's the same as or complementary to that used for the invitations. Print out the bride's and groom's first names on the computer or freehand onto white cardstock. Cut out the letters and mount one letter in the center of each circle with a glue stick. Punch two small holes at the top of each circle and thread a piece of fuchsia ribbon through the holes to hang.

take-out lunch
Your guests will love opening these pretty packages and discovering a delicious lunch.

Fill each cardboard gift bag (see Resources, page 94) with the menu items. To close, feed a 30" (76cm) length of fuchsia ribbon through the holes of the gift bag. Then, tie a bow over a red napkin and clear plastic fork.

menu

The menu and presentation of the food for this shower is both simple and uniquely decorative. Present guests with a decorated paper bag, filled with a pre-made lunch. Fill a party tub with a variety of orange, red and pink colored sodas for the guests to pick up along with their lunch (see Resources, page 94). Because you will want the lunch bags sitting out on the table before the guests arrive, have the guests eat at the beginning of the shower. Here are some suggestions for items to include in the lunch bags.

- Club or chicken salad sandwiches served on a Kaiser roll or sourdough bread (wrap sandwiches in white parchment paper and tie with a string for an added decorative element)
- Small bag of potato chips
- Broccoli Cheese Salad (*see recipe below*)
- Giant Gingersnap Cookies (*see recipe below*)

RECIPES

Broccoli Cheese Salad
SERVES 6

1 stalk fresh broccoli florets cut into small pieces

4 ounces Swiss cheese, cut into small cubes

4 ounces cheddar cheese, cut into small cubes

6 slices of bacon, cooked and crumbled

1 cup ranch dressing

1. Toss all of the ingredients to mix well. Place half-cup servings in small plastic containers and chill until ready to place in lunch bags.

Giant Gingersnaps
MAKES 24 COOKIES

4 cups all-purpose flour

2 teaspoons baking powder

1 teaspoon baking soda

1 teaspoon salt

2 teaspoons cinnamon

2 teaspoons ginger

1 teaspoon cloves

1½ cups butter or shortening

2 cups sugar

2 eggs

½ cup molasses

4 tablespoons granulated sugar

1. Preheat oven to 350° (177° C).

2. Sift flour, baking powder, baking soda, salt and spices together in a medium bowl; set aside.

3. Cream the butter and 2 cups sugar together in a large mixing bowl. Add eggs one at a time, mixing well after each addition. Add molasses and mix well. Blend the dry ingredients into the creamy mixture.

4. For each cookie, roll ¼ cup dough into a ball and roll each ball into granulated sugar. Place on cookie sheet about 3" (8cm) apart. Gently press down each cookie with the palm of your hand until dough is ¼" (1cm) thick. Bake for 12–15 minutes, until golden brown.

entertainment

Everyone loves getting involved in games at parties. Here are a couple of suggestions for entertaining your guests. You'll want to have some fun prizes ready to reward the winners of your games.

build-a-story game

Write a brief story of how the couple met and got engaged. Remove 10–12 words from the story, including a variety of nouns, verbs and adjectives. Give each guest a list of the kinds of words they need to write down (e.g. verb ending in "ing", kind of food, occupation) to fill in the blanks of the story (they do not see the story at this point in the game). Collect the completed word lists and read each story, replacing the removed words with each guest's new word list. The bride can choose which guest wins the prize for the most creative story. Below is a sample story and the accompanying word list you'd give to each guest.

> *Andrew and Emily met at (a dance) while they were (talking) and (laughing) with (friends). Andrew (noticed) Emily first and thought she was the most (beautiful) (girl) he had ever laid eyes on. They (quickly) fell (head over heels) for each other and neither one was at all (interested) in (dating) another (person) after that. Andrew (proposed) to Emily on a (rainy) (afternoon) at (his house). Emily (yelled) with (enthusiasm), "Of course I'll (marry) you!" The (happy) couple will be (married) on Saturday, May 20th and will then leave for their (romantic) honeymoon to (Italy).*

1. A place
2. Verb ending in "ing"
3. Verb ending in "ing"
4. Noun
5. Verb ending in "ed"
6. Adjective
7. Noun
8. Adverb
9. Romantic phrase
10. Adjective ending in "ed"
11. Verb ending in "ing"
12. Noun
13. Verb ending in "ed"
14. Adjective
15. Time of day
16. A place
17. Verb ending in "ed"
18. Expressive noun
19. Active verb
20. Adjective
21. Verb ending in "ed"
22. Adjective
23. A place

marriage memory game

Prepare memory cards with pictures of marriage-related words or phrases. Have guests take turns, turning over two cards at a time to try and find a match. Each time a player successfully turns over two matching cards, she will receive a candy bar that corresponds with that particular wedding word or phrase. Following is a list of card ideas with their matching candy bars.

Card Idea	Candy Bar
Bride	*Babe Ruth*
Groom	*Big Hunk*
Honeymoon	*Skor*
Budget	*Pay Day*
Ring	*Whoppers*
Lingerie	*Whatchamacallit*
Father of the bride	*Mr. Goodbar*
Marriage	*Rocky Road*
Gifts	*Good & Plenty*
"You may kiss the bride"	*Kisses*
Taking off the garter	*Butterfinger*
Bridesmaids	*3 Musketeers*
Throwing the bouquet	*Flipz*
Love	*Symphony*
Wedding expenses	*100 Grand*

Keepsake Ideas

As the hostess, your gift to the bride could be a keepsake clock personalized with the couple's names and wedding date. Set the clock out during the shower or present it to the bride as she opens her gifts.

candy tin favor

As the guests leave the shower, give them each one of these colorfully filled and decorated tins to take home. Buying jelly beans in a few specific colors (see Resources, page 94) is an easy and elegant way to coordinate this gift with the colors used in the invitations and decorations.

Fill a small glass-top silver tin with a custom mix of red, pink and orange jelly beans. Tie a bow around the tin with a piece of fuchsia ribbon and mount a "love" tag below the ribbon with a pop dot (a ¼" [6mm] thick foam circle with adhesive on both sides used to make elements visually "pop" off of the page in papercrafting).

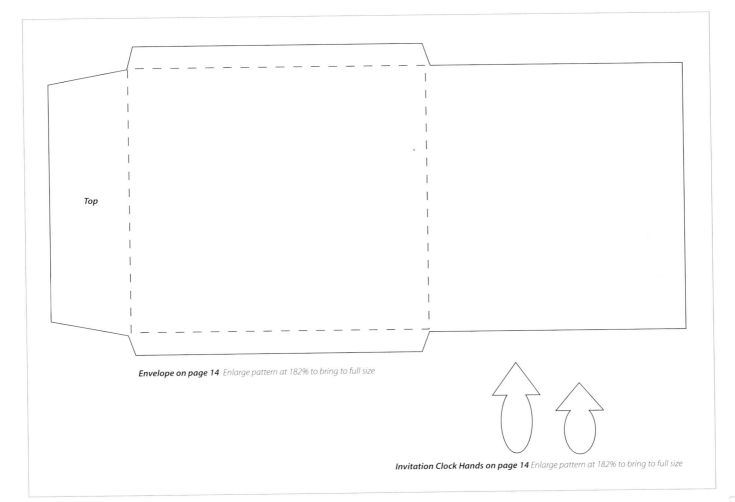

Top

Envelope on page 14 *Enlarge pattern at 182% to bring to full size*

Invitation Clock Hands on page 14 *Enlarge pattern at 182% to bring to full size*

Taking the Plunge

This delightful water theme plays upon the couple's exciting plunge into the world of marriage. Created for the active, fun-loving couple, this casual outdoor barbecue is an ideal opportunity for the couple to stock up on the kitchen and lawn items they'll need to host outdoor parties of their own once they've tied the knot. Hosting the party around a pool or water setting would be a terrific way to incorporate the water theme to its fullest potential. If a pool or other water setting is not available, however, convey the theme through the bubbly invitations and playful beach- and pool-inspired decorations.

Scott and Heather are taking the

PLUNGE!

Help the happy couple get started
out right
by attending a His and Hers shower
Saturday night
Something meant for him and something
meant for her
Items for the lawn and kitchen will
delight them, I'm sure

water bubbles invitation

Enveloped in bubbles, this invitation is the perfect way to prepare your guests for a fun-filled celebration. Since most showers are held for only the bride, it is important to clearly note in the invitation that this party is for both the bride and groom.

Gift Ideas

To carry this water theme even further, include a gift tag on the back of the invitation for each couple to use for their gift. Some scrapbook papers have coordinating tag sets that you can use for this purpose. If all of the guests use the gift tag as inspiration for their wrapping, the gifts would add a fun decorative accent to the party.

MATERIALS

12" × 12" (30cm × 30cm) blue bubbles vellum (SEI)

8½" × 11" (22cm × 28cm) piece of white cardstock

8½" × 11" (22cm × 28cm) piece of blue cardstock for circle tabs and pockets

custom gift tag

scissors

glue stick

bone folder

invitation sleeve pattern, at right

Invitation sleeve on this page Enlarge pattern at 200%, and enlarge again at 111% to bring to full size

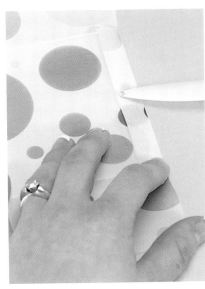

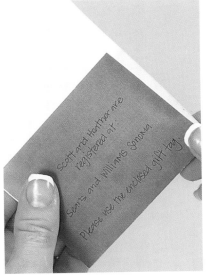

1. Glue the Sleeve Together

Cut a sleeve out of patterned vellum, using the pattern from page 22. Score and fold along the marked lines and adhere together with a glue stick.

2. Create the Invitation

Print the wording for the invitation in wavy lines on a 3⅞" × 7⅞" (10cm × 20cm) piece of white cardstock (see gift idea poem, page 26). Place other details in various sizes and colors of circles to match the bubbles on the vellum. To make the back pocket, cut a 3⅞" × 2½" (10cm × 6cm) piece of blue cardstock and glue the sides and bottom to the back of the invitation. Write the couple's registry information on the front of the pocket if you wish.

3. Insert the Invitation

Slide a custom gift tag into the pocket on the back of the invitation. Cut a small circle from the blue cardstock and glue it to the top of the invitation. Slide the finished invitation into the vellum sleeve.

decorations

A variety of blues, light green and white create an atmosphere of water that will make your guests feel as though they've plunged into an underwater world. Circles are used in much of the decorating to imitate bubbles. Use the following decorating suggestions to further play upon this water theme.

- Hang various sized round paper lanterns in blue, white and light green as a backdrop behind the serving area.
- Line the serving table with wheat grass centerpieces (see project at right).
- Place groups of blue, white and green helium-filled balloons around the party area.
- Scatter word pebbles around the serving area (see project on page 24).
- Make a sign, using the bubble theme, that says, "Scott and Heather are taking the plunge!"
- Place gifts in a small kiddy pool and set snorkels, fins and pool toys around the setting.

wheat grass and paint can centerpiece

Give your party area the feel of the beach with these wheat grass centerpieces.

To make them, cover a half-gallon paint can (see Resources, page 94) with scrapbook paper with a bubbles theme, using spray adhesive. Fill the can with either real or artificial wheat grass, inserted into floral foam. Trim the tops of the grass to be all the same height.

entertainment

The games suggested here will provide plenty of laughs for all of your guests. If you are hosting a party around a pool, swimming would be an obvious entertainment option—just be sure to inform your guests beforehand. Depending on the length of the shower and the number of guests invited, you may or may not have time to play both games as well as swim, so pick which one will work best for you.

"how well do you know me?" game

This game will allow guests to see just how well the bride and groom know each other. Prior to the shower, prepare a list of approximately five questions for the bride and groom to answer about one another separately. Include questions like, "What is Kim's favorite movie?" or "How does Joe like his eggs?" If you like, record each of them giving their answers on video to show later at the shower. This will capture their expressions as well as their unrehearsed answers.

At the shower, have the bride and groom answer the questions about themselves, and compare these answers to those given before the shower by their spouse-to-be. This game is meant as pure entertainment, hence no one will be awarded a prize at the end.

water balloon volleyball game

This is the perfect game for a hot summer day. Set up a volleyball net in an area that won't be harmed by water. Fill an ample supply of small, round water balloons. Divide the guests into two teams, keeping couples together. Give each couple a towel for catching and returning water balloons.

The game is played like volleyball, with each couple "serving" the water balloon across the net to any of the couples across the net, who then catch the balloon in their towel and launch it back over the net. When a couple drops a balloon they are eliminated from the game. The last couple left in the game wins a prize.

candy favor with word pebble magnet

Send each couple home with a pint-sized paint can filled with a custom mix of blue, green and white candy-coated chocolate candies (see Resources, page 94). Top off the can with a word pebble magnet.

To make the can, affix a piece of white paper to a pint-sized paint can (see Resources, page 94) using spray adhesive. Mount a piece of bubble-patterned vellum on top of the white paper using spray adhesive.

For the word pebble magnet, print a love-related word on white cardstock. Trace the shape of a large, blue picture pebble (see Resources, page 94) over one of the words and cut out. Mount the paper cutout on the back of the pebble, using an epoxy glue (Zap-A-Gap works very well). Press firmly for ten seconds. Then, mount a round, extra strong magnet to the back of the pebble, again using the epoxy glue. Place the magnet on the lid of the paint can to complete the party favor.

menu

The menu for this shower features traditional barbecue fare that is simple to prepare and works well for serving a large group of people. Apart from the Frothy Ocean Cooler, everything on the menu can be prepared in advance, so all you need to worry about is grilling the kabobs as your guests arrive.

Because this is a casual gathering, tables with place settings are unnecessary. Ample seating for everyone is all you need. If you plan to remain outdoors for the games, a circular seating arrangement works best.

- Shish Kabobs *(see recipe below)*
- Potato salad
- Corn on the cob
- Baked beans
- Frothy Ocean Cooler *(see recipe below)*
- Better-Than-Sex Cake *(see recipe below)*

RECIPES

Chicken and Sausage Shish Kabobs
SERVES 6-8

4 skinless, boneless chicken breasts, cut into 1½" (4cm) pieces

2 pounds (1 pound each) beef smoked sausage, cut into 1½" (4cm) chunks

2 large white onions, cut into chunks

1 pound baby portabella mushrooms

marinade of your choice

wooden or metal skewers

1. Place chicken pieces in a glass baking dish or large zippered plastic bag. Pour marinade over chicken, cover and refrigerate overnight.

2. Discard marinade. Skewer the meat and vegetables in alternating patterns. Grill kabobs over medium-low heat for 12 minutes and serve.

Better-Than-Sex Cake
SERVES 12

1 cup flour

½ cup butter, softened

1 cup chopped walnuts

1 8-ounce package cream cheese

1 cup sugar

12 ounces whipped topping, divided

1 package (4-serving size) instant chocolate pudding

1 package (4-serving size) instant vanilla pudding

3 cups cold milk

blue, white and light green M&M's

1. Preheat oven to 350° (177°C).

2. Mix first three ingredients and press into the bottom of a 9" × 13" (23cm × 33cm) pan. Bake for 15–20 minutes and cool.

3. Combine cream cheese, sugar and 6 ounces whipped topping with a mixer until smooth; spread over cooled crust.

4. Mix the two puddings and milk as directed on package to make pudding; spread over cream cheese layer.

5. Spread remaining 6 ounces of whipped topping over the pudding layer. Sprinkle the top with candy. Refrigerate until ready to serve.

Frothy Ocean Cooler
SERVES 16

1 gallon vanilla ice cream

1 gallon Bodacious Berry Hawaiian Punch

1. Place a generous scoop of vanilla ice cream in a plastic cup. Fill with punch and serve.

coaster set keepsake

This is a very fun and practical gift for the honored couple. Complete the keepsake before the shower using five photos of the bride and groom together.

MATERIALS

1 package of 3" (8cm) wooden discs, 6 discs total

6 black-and-white photos, printed on white cardstock

fine grit sandpaper

¼ yard (.23m) clear, soft plastic

dark blue eyelets

light blue eyelets

Brilliant Ultramarine acrylic paint (FolkArt)

ballpoint pen

⅛" (3mm) hole punch

½" (12mm) flat paintbrush

découpage medium

compass

scissors

craft knife

eyelet setter, hammer and mat

Gift Ideas

Since this is a couple's shower, gifts are intended for both the bride and the groom. While guests need not be assigned specific gifts, the invitation should clearly state that it is a lawn and kitchen shower. The guests can then decide how they want to incorporate that theme into their gift. Use the poem below to share the gift idea information in a fun and creative way.

"Help the happy couple get started out right

by attending a His and Hers Shower Saturday night.

Something meant for him, and something meant for her;

Items for the lawn and kitchen will delight them, I'm sure."

1. Paint the Discs

Using fine grit sandpaper, sand the wooden discs until smooth. Paint the bottoms and sides of the discs with Brilliant Ultramarine.

2. Cut Out the Photos

Use a compass to draw a 3" (8cm) circle around the couple in each picture and cut out. (Or print them in 3" [8cm] circles if using a computer.)

3. Adhere Photos to the Discs

Affix a photo to the unpainted side of each disc with découpage medium.

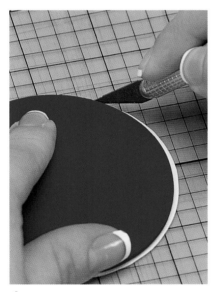

4. Trim Off Excess Paper

Trim any excess paper with a craft knife to make the coasters nice and neat.

5. Encase Discs in Plastic

Using a compass and a ballpoint pen, cut out two 4¼" (11cm) circles from the plastic for each coaster. Place one piece of plastic on either side of the disc and begin setting eyelets around the perimeter, setting them at opposite sides to keep the plastic taught. *(See Setting Eyelets, page 11.)*

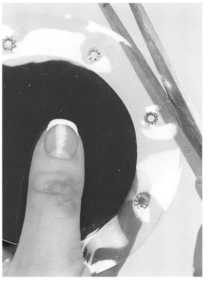

6. Continue Setting Eyelets

Alternating eyelet colors, continue setting eyelets for a total of eight on each coaster. Trim the plastic around the coasters to make even.

Fiesta, Mi Amor

Convey the passion and energy of a Mexican fiesta in this couple's dinner party. Although a nontraditional shower option, it's perfect for the couple that loves gathering with close friends in a personable, cozy setting. Everything about this shower is bright and festive—from the vibrant heart invitations and luminaries to the colorful serving set you paint yourself. And the romantic details infused into this fiesta are sure to elicit the same passionate feelings that brought the bride- and groom-to-be together.

fiesta heart invitation

The romantic heart motif on this invitation will let your guests know this fiesta is all about love. The papers and techniques used to create this card will be used again to create the festive luminaries (see project, page 32).

MATERIALS

white poster board cut to 6" × 8" (15cm × 20cm)

brightly colored tissue paper

mulberry paper, contrasting color to the tissue paper

scrapbook paper

wire

beads

paintbrush

glue stick

découpage medium

⅛" (3mm) hole punch

craft knife

bone folder

heart pattern, page 36

1. Spread découpage medium on one side of the poster board and cover with tissue paper. When dry, turn the poster board over, wrap the excess tissue around the edge and adhere with more découpage medium. When dry, fold the board in half and score, to create a 4" × 6" (10cm × 15cm) card.

2. Trace the heart pattern from page 36 onto the front of the card and cut out, using the craft knife. Punch the holes where indicated on the pattern. *(See Punching Holes, page 10.)*

3. Glue a piece of the mulberry paper over the back of the cutout. Line the entire inside of the invitation with a piece of scrapbook paper.

4. Print the invitation wording on white paper and glue inside.

5. Near the score line, punch a hole ½" (1cm) from the top and from the bottom. Add a wire embellishment with beads. Score a fold line ½" (1cm) from the spine on the invitation front. *(See Scoring and Folding Paper, page 10.)*

6. Using the envelope pattern on page 37, create an envelope for the finished invitation from the same paper that lines the inside of the card.

decorations

Brightly colored decorations, lively salsa music and plenty of appetizing Mexican food will help to create a vibrant and inviting atmosphere for your guests. Most of the decorating ideas for this shower center around the dinner table, since the majority of the party will be spent eating. You will find plenty of fiesta-themed decorations at party stores, but include a few unique elements as well, such as the handmade luminaries, to add a little more passion to the mix. Here are some additional suggestions for setting the mood.

- Luminaries lining the center of the table *(see project, page 32)*
- Painted terra cotta pots for the serving pieces *(see project, page 34)*
- Brightly colored red, orange or yellow tablecloths

- A brightly colored table runner
- Beaded napkin rings and place cards *(see project below)*
- Bulb lights hanging above the table
- Chili peppers
- Paper flowers

If you have a gift table or another area you would like to decorate, carry over some of the decorations from the list above and add a piñata hanging above the table, if this is one of your entertainment choices. You could also cover the table with a Mexican blanket.

napkin rings *These festive napkin rings use scraps of paper left over from the luminary project on page 32. Using scraps from the tissue-covered poster board saves time, paper and ensures that everything is perfectly coordinated.*

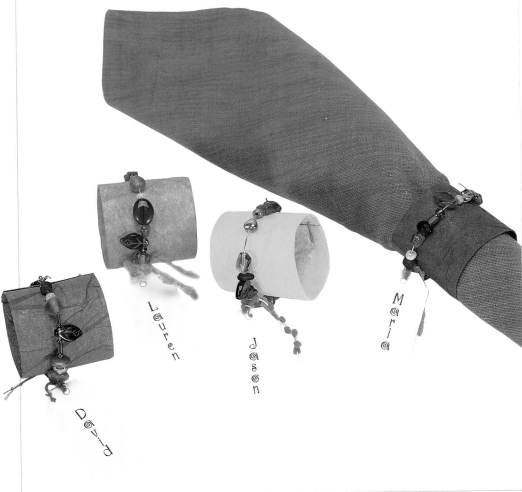

MATERIALS

5" × 1½" (13cm x 4cm) scrap piece of tissue-covered poster board (left over from luminary project on page 32)

white cardstock

assortment of small glass beads

24-gauge wire

brightly colored string

⅛" (3mm) hole punch

scissors

stapler

wire cutter

1. Overlap the ends of the strip of poster board and staple together.

2. String beads onto a 6" (15cm) piece of wire and twist the ends together, forming a circle.

3. Print each guest's name on a piece of cardstock and cut into a small tag.

4. Punch a hole in the top of the tag and attach to the beaded ring with string. Slide the beaded ring over the poster board ring.

luminary

Hand lanterns such as these were traditionally used in Mexico to light the way for the groom on his journey from his home to the home of the bride the night before the wedding. Used as decorations, these luminaries add a festive touch to the serving or dining tables at your celebration dinner.

MATERIALS

14" × 14" (36cm × 36cm) white poster board

brightly colored tissue paper

1 piece mulberry specialty paper (contrasting color from tissue paper)

scrap aluminum flashing

fine-gauge wire

assortment of brightly colored beads

⅛" (3mm) metal eyelets

votive candle and holder

découpage medium, matte finish

craft glue

eyelet setter, hammer and mat

sponge brush

⅛" (3mm) hole punch

craft knife

ruler

bone folder

1. Cover the Poster Board

Cover the 14" × 14" (36cm × 36cm) piece of poster board with découpage medium, using a sponge brush. Working in small sections, lay a piece of tissue paper over the glue and press flat, leaving a wrinkled appearance. Fold the excess tissue paper over onto the back of the board and glue down. Repeat the same process for the other side of the board.

2. Cut Out the Heart

Give both sides of the covered board another coat of découpage medium and let dry. Measure and cut out the luminary, using the pattern on page 37. Trace the heart pattern onto two opposite sides of the luminary and cut out, using a craft knife.

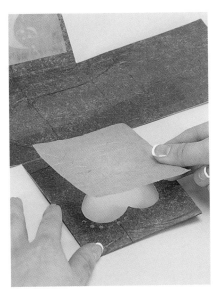

3. Add the Mulberry Paper

Score the four sides of the luminary with a bone folder. Use the small hole punch to outline part of the heart where indicated on the template. Glue a piece of mulberry paper to the back of each heart.

4. Cut Out Metal Strips

Cut four ¼" × 4½" (2cm × 11cm) strips of aluminum, and fold them in half lengthwise. Punch a hole ¼" (6mm) down from the tops and bottoms of the strips. Use the holes as a guide to mark the placement of the holes on the edges of the luminary.

5. Set Eyelets in the First Half

Using the eyelet setting tool and hammer, set an eyelet in one side of the top and bottom of each metal strip and fasten to one side of each luminary flap.

6. Glue the Other Half

Set the eyelets, only in the aluminum, on the opposite side of each metal strip. Using craft glue, adhere the other half of the strips to the luminary.

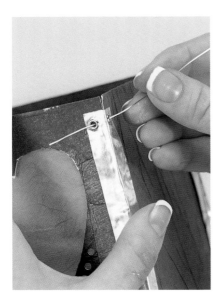

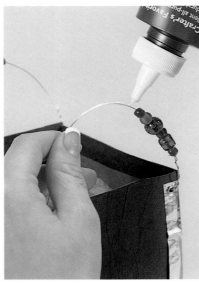

7. Secure the Corners

String a piece of wire through the top two eyelets of one corner on the luminary, and twist the wire on one side to hold it in place.

8. Glue the Beads

Thread some large and small colored beads onto the wire and thread the free end of the wire through the two holes on the opposite side of the luminary. Twist the wire to hold in place. Repeat for the other side of the luminary. Place a drop of craft glue on the top of each wire handle and slide a bead over the glue. Hold it in place until the glue dries. Place a votive candle inside the luminary and light.

painted serving pieces
Terra cotta pots of all sizes and shapes make perfect accessories to your wedding shower. Here the pots are used as serving pieces. To make them, paint all of the terra cotta pieces a variety of bright colors using acrylic paint. Try different painting techniques, such as color-washing (mixing water with the paint for a thin glaze of color) and crackling (using crackling medium, available at craft stores), for a variety of looks on your terra cotta pots. To use the pots as serving pieces, line them with aluminum foil or plastic wrap and fill. If you're having fajitas, as suggested on page 35, fill smaller pots with toppings and larger pieces with tortilla chips.

menu

Don't be intimidated by the idea of throwing a dinner party for 12–14 guests. A Mexican fajita dinner is an easy meal to create for a large group and it appeals to everyone's tastes. If the guest list grows much larger than seven or eight couples, you may want to adjust to a buffet-type dinner or serve only appetizers and dessert. Here are some menu ideas you may wish to consider preparing for this festive occasion.

- Chips and salsa *(see recipe below)*
- Grilled chicken and steak fajitas *(see recipe below)*
- Refried beans
- Spanish rice
- Frozen daiquiris or piña coladas
- Sopapillas with ice cream

For a fitting presentation, use the painted terra cotta pieces *(see project, page 34)* as the containers for the fajita toppings. Use a medium-sized pot for salsa and small pots for cheese (you may want to have two pots of cheese), onions, sour cream, guacamole, red peppers and green peppers. Place the small pots inside of a tray, and set on a lazy Susan to allow your guests easy access to the toppings. Serve chips in a larger bowl.

RECIPES

Mild Salsa
SERVES 6–8

3 large tomatoes
1 small yellow or white onion
1 medium carrot
1 bunch of cilantro
1 lime
garlic salt
pepper
jalapeño *(if desired)*

1. Peel the tomatoes, onion and carrot.

2. Grate the tomatoes on the large side of a cheese grater over a large bowl to form the base of the salsa.

3. Grate the onion on the large side of the grater.

4. Add the carrot by grating it on the small side of the grater.

5. Chop the cilantro as finely as possible and mix into the salsa.

6. Squeeze the juice from one lime into the salsa and mix.

7. Season with garlic salt, pepper and jalapeño to desired taste. Chill in refrigerator overnight.

Fajitas
SERVES 6

1 tablespoon chili powder
½ teaspoon salt
½ teaspoon paprika
1 teaspoon cumin
2 tablespoons cornstarch
1 tablespoon minced, dried onion
2 tablespoons sugar
½ to 1 teaspoon red pepper flakes
  (according to taste)
½ cup water
½ cup fresh lime juice
4 boneless, skinless chicken breasts
2–3 boneless top sirloin steaks
8" (20cm) flour tortillas

1. Mix the first six ingredients together in a medium bowl for the marinade. Add the sugar and red pepper flakes. Stir in the water and lime juice. Place the chicken and beef in separate zippered plastic bags or glass baking dishes. Pour marinade over the meat, cover and refrigerate overnight.

2. Grill the meat over medium heat until cooked throughout.

3. Cut the chicken and steak into thin strips and serve with desired toppings.

Toppings

cheddar cheese, shredded
guacamole
salsa
caramelized onions
sautéed red, green and yellow peppers
jalapeños
sour cream

entertainment

Since this is a dinner party, a majority of the shower will be spent eating dinner, but you should provide some activities for your guests as well. The Thirteen Coins game is played around the table, so it's perfect for when dinner is complete. You can set the stage for this fiesta by playing salsa music in the background and by leaving room for some Latin dancing. Or fill a piñata with gold-covered chocolate coins to get your guests up and about.

thirteen coins game

The inspiration for this game comes from a Mexican wedding tradition where the groom gives the bride thirteen gold coins as a symbol of his unquestionable trust and commitment to her. He then gives her a small chest or keepsake box in which to place the coins, signifying wealth and strength. In the Christian tradition, the thirteen coins represent Christ and his Twelve Apostles.

Adapting this tradition for the party, the host would place a golden heart charm under each of the guest's plates at dinner. Attached to each charm would be a small paper tag with a wish for the couple. Here is a sample list, or as the guests arrive, have them write their own, personalized wishes for the bride and groom.

- A happy home
- Unconditional love
- Trust
- Health and longevity

- Prosperity
- Peace
- Blessed with children
- Travel and adventure

- A strong, intimate relationship
- A lifetime of joy

At the conclusion of dinner, all of the guests would read their wishes and give their charms to the bride and groom. Because the number is set at 13, you will have to adjust according to your guest list. If you have fourteen guests, including the bride and groom, the host or hostess could read two of the wishes. If there are more than 14 guests, you may have each couple read one wish instead of each guest. If you do not want to keep the Christian symbolism of this tradition, the number of charms given does not matter. The charms could then be incorporated into a keepsake box or album for the bride and groom.

Gift Ideas

The Thirteen Gold Coins theme can be incorporated into other parts of the shower as well. When you send the invitations, explain the significance of the coins, then assign each guest (or couple) one of the wishes listed above. Ask that they incorporate the wish for the bride- and groom-to-be into the gift they are giving. For instance, if the guest is assigned the wish of peace, they could give the bride and groom a relaxation gift set that might include massage oil, bubble bath and bathrobes.

Heart for Invitation and Luminary on pages 30 and 32 *Copy pattern at 100%*

mini photo album keepsake

Incorporate the heart charms from the dinner into a mini photo album keepsake for the bride and groom. As the bride- and groom-to-be begin to fill the pages with photos from their married life, they will remember the festive way that their friends wished them blessings for their future together.

Begin with a pre-made mini album. Attach each charm and wish to one of the pages using a gold eyelet through the hole of the charm. Save one charm to decorate the outside of the album. String it on ribbon and thread it through the entire album. Place photos of the bride and groom on each page, or leave the pages blank for the couple to fill in with wedding or honeymoon photos. To help your guests remember this fiesta shower, present each with a small box or bag filled with thirteen gold chocolate coins. Decorate the box or bag in the vibrant colors of the fiesta.

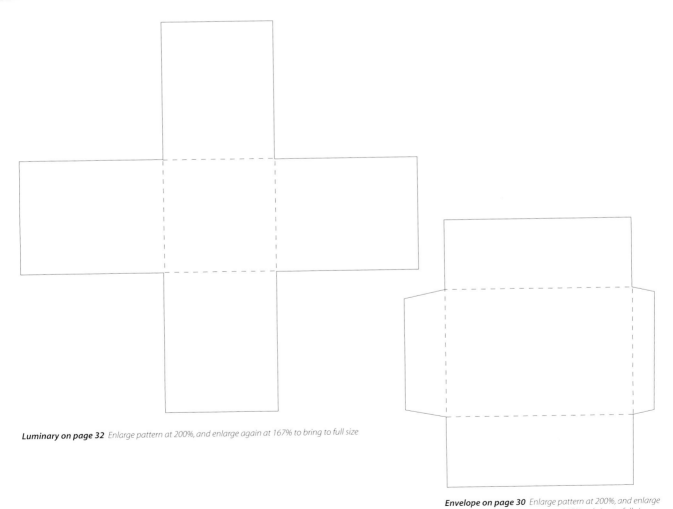

Luminary on page 32 Enlarge pattern at 200%, and enlarge again at 167% to bring to full size

Envelope on page 30 Enlarge pattern at 200%, and enlarge again at 167% to bring to full size

Sugar and Spice

Filled with homey details, the recipe for this shower is sure to whip up a successful celebration. The apron invitation sets the stage for a shower that gives guests the chance to share their favorite recipes with the bride-to-be, and maybe even a "sugar" or "spice" story about the happy couple. Whether she is already a cooking aficionado or needs help getting started, the memories created during this shower are sure to follow the bride-to-be into her own kitchen once she is married.

kitchen apron invitation

Your guests will love opening their mini apron invitation to find a recipe for fun and fellowship—a shower for a special bride-to-be!

Sugar 'N Spice
and...
sharp-cutting knives
and...
bowls and plates
and...
a tool that grates,
and...
everything else Kate needs for her new kitchen.

Please follow the recipe on the back of this card.

Recipe for: Kate's Kitchen Bridal Shower

Ingredients:
1 anxious bride-to-be
1 stressed-out mother of the bride
14 fabulous friends
1 c. fun
2 Tbl. laughter

Directions:
Combine all of the ingredients at 11:00 a.m. on August 23 and enjoy!

Please share a favorite recipe of yours with Kate by filling out the enclosed recipe card and then bring the cooked dish to our party.

invitation poem

Sugar 'N Spice
and...
sharp-cutting knives
and...
bowls and plates
and...
a tool that grates,
and...
everything else Kate needs for her new kitchen.

Please follow the recipe on the back of this card.

invitation recipe

Recipe for:
Kate's Kitchen Bridal Shower

Ingredients:
1 anxious bride-to-be
1 stressed-out mother of the bride
14 fabulous friends
1 c. fun
2 Tbl. laughter

Directions:
Combine all of the ingredients at 11:00 a.m. on August 23 and enjoy!

Please share a favorite recipe of yours with Kate by filling out the enclosed recipe card and then bring the cooked dish to our party.

MATERIALS

12" × 12" (30cm × 30cm) burgundy cardstock

8½" × 11" (22cm × 28cm) brown flecked cardstock

blank recipe cards

2 cinnamon sticks

6 antique metal eyelets

8" (20cm) length of jute

off-white embroidery floss

glue stick

large needle

⅛" (3mm) hole punch

eyelet setter, hammer and mat

scissors

apron invitation pattern, page 45

1. Using the template on page 45, cut out the apron shape and pocket from burgundy cardstock. Print the apron label on brown cardstock and trim to 2⅛" × 1⅛" (5cm × 4cm). Sew the label to the pocket piece with off-white embroidery thread. Use the needle to poke a few holes ahead of where you are sewing to help with the thread placement.

2. Place a narrow strip of glue around the sides and bottom edges of the back of the pocket with a glue stick and glue to the bottom of the apron. Use the hole punch to make a hole in each of the four corners of the pocket and in the two top corners of the apron. Set an eyelet in each of the holes.

3. Thread a piece of jute through the eyelets at the top of the apron to create the neck string; tie and knot the ends.

4. Print the invitation poem and the invitation recipe *(see right)* side-by-side on a piece of brown cardstock. Trim the cardstock to 4⅝" × 5½" (12cm × 14cm) and fold it in half so the printed sides are on the outside. Slide the folded invitation and a blank recipe card (for the guests to write down their favorite recipe) into the apron pocket. Insert a couple of small cinnamon sticks into the pocket for a finishing touch.

decorations

Use old-fashioned, country-style items for creating the atmosphere of this shower.

- Cover the serving table with an old quilt.
- Place wildflowers or sunflowers in Mason jars throughout the room.
- Paint a papier mâché canister to match the party theme, then fill with a variety of kitchen utensils. Place it on a table by the sitting area for the Kitchen Utensil Game *(see page 43)*.
- Place the muffin mix party favor bags *(see page 42)* on a table or in a large basket by the sitting area.

- Create a banner with the words "Sugar and Spice" by painting wooden letters a crimson red color and suspending them from a grapevine with twine or jute. Add kitchen utensils and ribbon ties to the grapevine for more details.
- If the bride has already decided on a decorating scheme for her new kitchen, you may want to incorporate her style and color choices into the party décor.

menu

In keeping with the cooking theme, ask each of your guests to bring a favorite recipe to share for a potluck meal. To avoid having too many dishes of one course, assign each guest to bring a main dish, side dish or dessert. As the hostess, you may want to provide the beverage and a variety of breads to complement the main dishes.

- Potluck meal
- Raspberry Lemonade *(see recipe below)*

- Breads, including cornbread and Honey Butter *(see recipe below)*

RECIPES

Laurie's Raspberry Lemonade
SERVES 4–6

½ cup fresh lemon juice

¾ cup frozen raspberries

¾ cup sugar

3 cups cold water

1. Blend all of the ingredients in a blender until the raspberries are thoroughly chopped. Chill in refrigerator until ready to serve.

Honey Butter

½ cup butter, softened

⅓ cup honey

1. Use a mixer to whip the butter and honey together until smooth and fluffy.

muffin mix favor

Continue the kitchen theme by sending each guest home with a cooking mix and recipe. Place the mix in this cute muslin bag that's decorated to match the party invitations.

To make the bag for the muffin mix, cut a 6" × 16" (15cm × 41cm) piece of muslin fabric, fold it in half and sew up the sides with a ½" (1cm) seam. Leave the top unfinished, and turn the bag inside out, so the seams are on the inside. Print the label for the bag on a piece of muslin fabric *(see step 3 on page 44 for the technique for printing on muslin)*, then attach the label to a larger piece of plaid fabric using a needle and embroidery thread. Sew the finished label to the muslin bag with large stitches. Fill a plastic bag with the muffin mix and close with a twist tie. Slide the plastic bag inside the muslin bag and tie shut with a piece of jute. Attach the instructions card and slide a cinnamon stick through the jute.

Sugar 'n Spice Muffin Mix

MAKES 1 FAVOR

1 ¾ cups flour

2 tablespoons sugar

3 teaspoons baking powder

½ teaspoon baking soda

1 teaspoon ground cinnamon

½ teaspoon ground nutmeg

¼ teaspoon ground ginger

¼ teaspoon ground cloves

½ teaspoon salt

1. Combine all the ingredients in a medium bowl. Store the mixture in an airtight container if not placing in the bags right away.

2. Attach the following instructions to the bag:

Sugar 'n Spice Muffins
Makes 1 dozen

Combine muffin mix with ¼ c. melted butter, 1 egg, 1 tsp. vanilla and 1 c. milk. Fill 12 greased muffin tins ⅔ full, and bake at 400° (204° C) for 15 minutes.

Thank you for adding your Spice to Kate's bridal shower.

Gift Ideas

Have each guest tell a "Sugar" (something sweet) or "Spice" (something not so sweet) experience about the bride or groom as the bride opens up her gift. Have someone record the experiences for the bride to keep.

entertainment

Both of the games for this shower are meant to entertain as well as provide the bride with items she needs for her new kitchen. To continue your kitchen theme, give the winners a cookbook or gourmet food items.

guess the spice game

Cover the labels on a variety of spice bottles and number the bottles. Provide each guest with a piece of paper and pencil. Pass the spices around and allow the guests to smell and look at each spice. Have them write down their guess as to the identity of each spice. The person who correctly guesses the most spices wins a prize. Then give the collection of spices to the bride for her kitchen.

kitchen utensil collection game

Interview the groom before the party, asking him a variety of questions about himself. Prepare at least as many questions as there will be guests. The questions might include, "What is your favorite meal?" or "What personality trait do you love most about your fiancée?"

Write the questions on a piece of paper and attach the paper to a kitchen utensil. Have each guest draw one of the utensils from a canister and have her read the question to the bride. If the bride's answer matches the groom's, the bride receives the kitchen utensil. If she is wrong, the guest keeps the utensil.

recipe box keepsake

A wonderful keepsake for the bride-to-be is a collection of recipes gathered from the friends who attend her shower. Slide an empty recipe card in the apron of the invitation and ask each guest to write down one of her favorite recipes on the blank card. Follow the instructions on page 44 for making the recipe box, and fill it with the collected recipe cards, as well as a supply of blank cards for the bride to fill in later on.

MATERIALS

wood recipe box (Walnut Hollow)

mini wooden rolling pin

burgundy cardstock

natural kraft cardstock

scrap of plaid fabric

scrap of muslin fabric

12 antique metal eyelets

4 small buttons

1 large button

10" (25cm) of twine

crimson embroidery thread

off-white embroidery thread

Napthol Crimson acrylic paint (FolkArt)

Licorice acrylic paint (FolkArt)

fine-grit sand paper

½" (12mm) flat brush

glue gun and glue

eyelet setter, hammer and mat

large needle

ruler

1. Prepare the Box

Sand the recipe box with fine-grit sandpaper and wipe clean with a damp cloth.

2. Basecoat the Box

Basecoat the entire outside of the box with Napthol Crimson, using the ½" (12mm) brush. Paint the rolling pin handles with the same color. After the paint has dried, water down a puddle of Licorice paint to an inky consistency and lightly stroke over the crimson paint, just enough to give an aged appearance.

3. Create the Tag

Print the wording on a piece of muslin fabric by taping the fabric to a piece of cardstock and running it through an ink-jet printer. Hand-sew a piece of printed muslin to a larger piece of plaid fabric with red embroidery thread.

4. Add the Buttons

Sew a small button in each corner of the plaid fabric, using off-white thread.

5. Measure the Twine

Hot glue a large button to the front of the recipe box, just below where the lid and the box meet. Measure a piece of twine around the button to determine how much slack to leave. Don't pull it too tightly around the button or you will not be able to slide it back over the button once the twine is glued down.

6. Adhere the Twine

Using the glue gun, glue the two ends of the twine beneath where the fabric label will go.

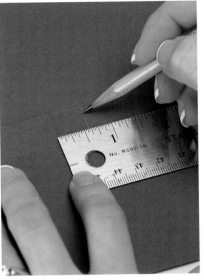

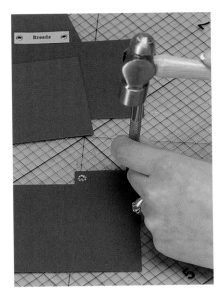

7. Adhere the Label and Rolling Pin

Hot glue the fabric label in the center of the lid. Hot glue the mini rolling pin to the top right corner of the label. To finish the box, lightly sand the edges of the box to give it a distressed look.

8. Create Divider Cards

Cut six 3½" × 5" (9cm × 13cm) divider cards out of the burgundy cardstock. Cut a 1¼" (4cm) tab out of the top of the card. Space each preceding tab about ⅝" (2cm) past the previous tab.

9. Print the Labels

Print the divider labels on natural brown cardstock and cut down to 1⅛" × ⁷⁄₁₆" (4cm × 1cm). Attach the labels to the tabs with antique metal eyelets.

Apron Pocket on page 40 *Enlarge pattern at 167% to bring to full size*

10. Print the Recipe Cards

Print generic recipe cards on kraft cardstock and cut down to 3" × 5" (8cm × 13cm). Arrange in the recipe box.

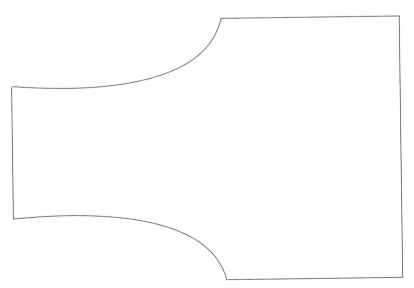

Apron Invitation on page 40 *Enlarge pattern at 167% to bring to full size*

Luxury Bridal Spa

Preparing for a wedding is stressful for almost every bride at some point along the way. This shower gives her a little time to relax and rejuvenate her mind and body before the big day. A calm atmosphere, good food and fun conversation with her closest family and friends make this mini-spa experience one any bride will remember as a welcome release. And to help ensure you have a relaxing day too, enlist two or three other attendees to help coordinate the facials and foot scrubs and serve the smoothies.

come be
PAMPERED

SPA SHOWER

Join us in pampering the bride at a spa
bridal shower for Claire Lewis

Friday, April 23
6:00 pm

at the home of Jennifer Harker
153 S. Meadowbrook Dr.
Ashville, North Carolina

Please R.S.V.P. by April 13 at 555-5555.

bath salts invitation

Let the pampering experience begin before the shower even starts! This invitation includes a small handmade envelope filled with lavender bath salts that bears the phrase "Come be pampered" on the outside. Who could resist an invitation that serves as a small gift as well?

MATERIALS

12" × 12" (30cm × 30cm) handmade lavender paper

12" × 12" (30cm × 30cm) white cardstock

8½" × 11" (22cm × 28cm) white cardstock

ink-jet sticker paper

small cellophane bag

lavender ribbon

lavender bath salts

dried lavender

craft glue

⅛" (3mm) hole punch

craft knife

ruler

invitation pattern, page 53

Tip

A huge variety of fonts are available for download on the Internet. The font I used here is Gingersnap, downloaded from www.twopeasinabucket.com. Look up type fonts in any search engine to see an amazing array of options. There is sure to be a font perfect for your shower.

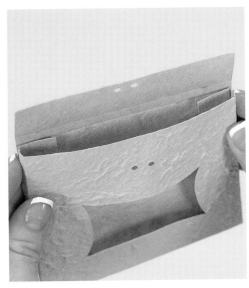

1. Create the Envelope

Use the template on page 53 to make an envelope out of the lavender paper. Cut the window out of the front panel, as marked, using a craft knife. Fold the envelope as indicated on the template and glue the sides to the back panel, using craft glue. Punch two holes where shown on the template, using a small hole punch.

2. Fill Bags with Salts

Fill the cellophane bag with 3 tablespoons of lavender bath salts, then press the salts to flatten the package. Trim off the top of the bag, leaving about 1½" (4cm) of bag above the salts.

3. Print the Invitation

Print the invitation information onto white cardstock, then cut it down to 3⅝" × 3⅝" (9cm × 9cm). Slide the invitation and the bag of salts into the lavender envelope, making sure the bag shows through the window. Print "Come Be Pampered" on the stickers in lavender ink. Center the sticker over the fold of the cellophane bag centered in the envelope window.

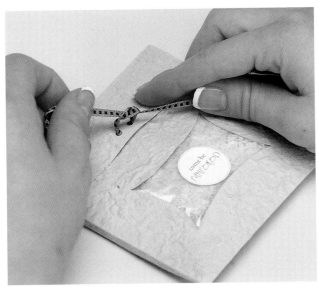

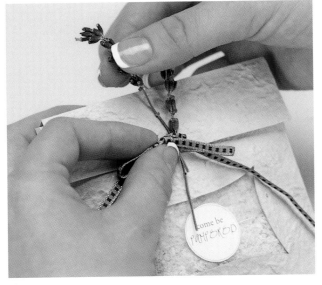

4. Tie the Invitation Closed

Thread a piece of ribbon through the holes in the envelope and tie a bow.

5. Tuck in Lavender

Tuck a couple of dried lavender sprigs through the knot of the bow to finish.

decorations

The decorations for this shower should create a soothing atmosphere that will allow the bride and her guests to relax and unwind. Using a color scheme of lavender and sage green will add to the calm setting of this party.

- Display groups of various sized sage and lavender candles around the room. Set the candles in lavender candlescaping gravel.
- Place arrangements of dried or fresh lavender around the room.
- Wrap white hand towels with lavender ribbon and place in a basket or wooden box to be used when you do the facial masks.
- Spread bath salts and dried lavender around the serving table.
- Play soothing music or nature sounds in the background to create a relaxing atmosphere.

menu

In keeping with a spa atmosphere, the food for this shower is healthy but tasty. Most of the food can be left out for the guests to snack on in between their spa treatments and the other shower activities.

- Turkey wraps on sun-dried tomato tortillas
- Hummus dip with pita wedges *(see recipe below)*
- Vegetable platter
- Cucumber, tomato, feta cheese salad
- Berry Smoothies *(see recipe below)*
- Bottled water

RECIPES

Hummus Dip

1 cup chickpeas, soaked and cooked

3 cloves garlic, minced

3 tablespoons lemon juice

¼ cup water

3 tablespoons tahini *(sesame paste)*

½ to 1 teaspoon cumin

½ teaspoon paprika

1. Mix chickpeas, garlic, lemon juice and water in a food processor for about 1 minute. Stir in the tahini and spices. Chill in refrigerator.

Pita Wedges

10–12 pita bread pockets

4 tablespoons olive oil

2 tablespoons paprika

salt

pepper

1. Preheat the oven to 375° (191℃). Brush olive oil over each side of the pita bread and sprinkle with paprika, salt and pepper. Cut pita bread into wedges and place on a baking sheet. Bake for 8–10 minutes.

2. Cool, then store in an airtight container. Serve with hummus dip.

Berry Smoothies
SERVES 3–4

1 cup frozen strawberries or raspberries

½ cup frozen blackberries

1 cup vanilla frozen yogurt

¼ cup frozen orange juice concentrate

1½ cups milk

1. Blend all ingredients to desired consistency. Prepare the smoothies before the shower and place in the freezer. Remove the smoothies from the freezer as guests start arriving to thaw some before serving. Serve the smoothies to the guests as they are waiting for the facial mask treatment or foot scrub treatment to dry.

entertainment

The activities for this shower will allow your guests to relax but still have fun in the company of friends and family. Guests can participate in two spa treatments, a facial mask and a foot and hand scrub, at their leisure during the shower. To make sure everyone has time for each treatment, have half the guests do the facial treatment first, while the other half applies the foot and hand scrub.

As they wait for their treatments to dry, they can eat and chat with one another while playing the Wedding Word Blackout game.

facial masks

Prepare two or three homemade facial masks before the shower begins *(see recipes below)*. As the guests arrive, have them wash their faces with a facial wipe (available in a variety of brands) and choose a mask to apply. The Banana Moisture Mask is ideal for guests with dry skin, while the Avocado Mask is for guests with oily skin.

Once the masks are applied, invite the guests to relax for 15–20 minutes to allow their masks to dry. When the guests are ready to wash off their masks, hand them a towel and washcloth that have been rolled together with ribbon.

Banana Moisture Mask

1 ripe banana, mashed

1 tablespoon honey

1 tablespoon plain yogurt

Avocado Mask

1 egg white

1 teaspoon lemon juice

½ avocado pulp, mashed

1. Mix ingredients and apply to face. Allow mask to dry on face for 15–20 minutes.

foot and hand scrub

The next spa treatment the guests will receive is to take care of their hands and feet. Prepare a foot and hand scrub for each guest before the shower begins *(see recipe below)*. Have on hand a plastic basin filled with warm water for each guest. To make it easier, have half of the guests do the facial treatment first, while the other half applies the foot and hand scrub and then switch, refilling the water basins with fresh water.

As the bride and shower guests relax with the foot and hand scrub treatment, serve them smoothies to drink.

1 tablespoon of coarse, clean sand

¼ cup light canola oil

¼ cup liquid hand soap

¼ cup sea salt

¼ cup Epsom salt

1. Mix all of the ingredients and soak feet or hands for 10 minutes.

wedding word blackout game

Prior to the shower date, prepare necklaces using lavender ribbon and a small washer imprinted with wedding-related words *(see Resources, page 94)* for each guest. Choose one of the words to make off limits for anyone to say during the shower. As each guest arrives, give her a necklace and tell her what word cannot be said during the shower. A person can steal a necklace from another individual when she hears her say the word. The person with the most necklaces at the end of the shower wins a prize.

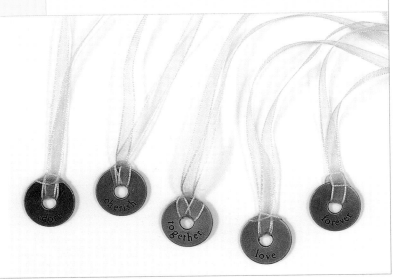

lavender soap favor

The pampering continues even after the shower as you send each guest home with a handmade bar of lavender-vanilla soap.

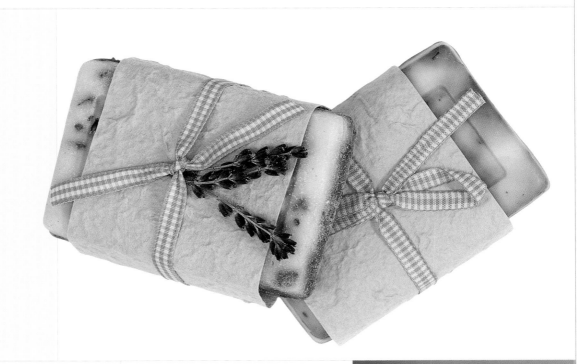

MATERIALS

purple handmade paper

⅛" (3mm) wide purple and white ribbon

white glycerin soap

vanilla essential oil

lavender essential oil

dried lavender buds

dried lavender stems

glue stick

soap mold

scissors

1. Following the manufacturer's instructions, melt a package of white glycerin soap. Add a teaspoon of dried lavender buds, 3 drops of vanilla essential oil and 3 drops of lavender essential oil to the melted soap.

2. Fill the mold with the melted soap to ¼" (6mm) from the top. Allow the soap to cool in the mold for about 5 minutes then cover with lavender buds. Fill the rest of the mold with melted glycerin.

3. Once the soap has set, wrap the soap with a piece of handmade paper, securing the ends with a glue stick. Tie with a ribbon, then slip a stem of dried lavender into the knot.

memories album keepsake

Help the bride remember this mini-spa experience by preparing a mini album for her to fill with photos of herself and her friends from the night. Decorate each page of the album with photo corners, picture mattes, dried lavender and page titles. and allow the bride to fill the album with her favorite photos from the party. Set aside one or two pages for each guest to sign during the shower.

Gift Ideas

To make the gifts the guests bring even more special, have the individual who gave the gift also give a piece of advice for the bride as she opens the gift. These responses could be written in the bride's keepsake album.

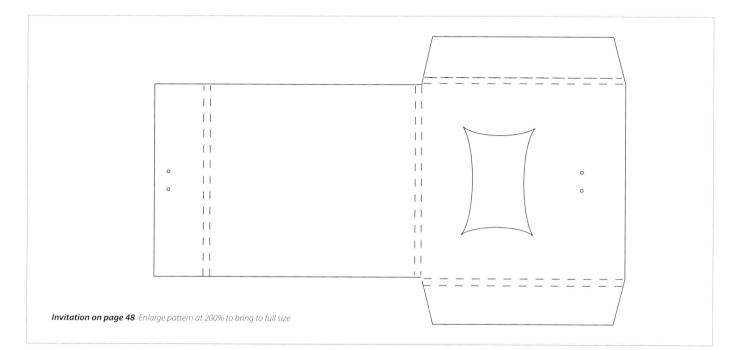

Invitation on page 48 *Enlarge pattern at 200% to bring to full size*

Something Borrowed, Something Blue

A Victorian-themed wedding shower is a fitting celebration
for a bride-to-be who loves romance, elegance and refinement.
Family and tradition were important aspects of the Victorian Era,
so this shower is a perfect gathering for close family and friends.
A sit-down brunch with formal place settings would work nicely for
a gathering of eight to sixteen guests, while a buffet-style brunch
might work better for a larger group. During warm months, an
outdoor flower garden would make a beautiful setting for this
shower, while a formal dining room or living room works nicely in
cooler months.

Victorian charm invitation

This lovely handmade invitation captures the elegance and style that were so much a part of the Victorian Era. The paper doily inside the invitation adds the perfect Victorian touch.

MATERIALS

- 12" × 12" (30cm × 30cm) blue/green roses scrapbook paper
- 12" × 12" (30cm × 30cm) light blue cardstock
- small paper doily
- "Something Old, Something New..." stamp (All Night Media)
- thin blue ribbon
- small Victorian heart charm
- blue ink stamp pad
- spray glue adhesive
- clear embossing powder
- bone folder
- heat tool
- ruler
- scissors

1. Prepare the Cardstock

Cut the blue cardstock to 4⅝" × 10" (12cm × 25cm), and print the wording for the invitation on one side. Cut a piece of the roses paper to 4⅜" × 9¾" (11cm × 25cm) and mount on the unprinted side of the blue cardstock with spray adhesive; smooth out all the bubbles.

2. Score the Card

Using the bone folder and ruler, score a line 4½" (11cm) from the top of the invitation and fold over to crease. Score a second line along the edge where the top flap meets the cardstock. Fold and crease the bottom flap.

3. Stamp the Phrase

Stamp the "Something Old..." phrase in the center of the small doily and sprinkle the wet ink with clear embossing powder. Tap off the excess powder onto a piece of scrap paper.

4. Melt the Powder

Using the heating tool, melt the embossing powder.

5. Add the Doily

Glue the doily to the top of the inside of the card.

6. Tie On the Heart Charm

Thread the heart charm onto the length of ribbon. With the heart charm at the bottom of the card, tie a bow around the outside of the invitation.

decorations

Victorian-style decorating can be described as elegant, lavish, eclectic and even a little cluttered. An abundance of flowers and lace will take you a long way in your decorating for this shower. You may also want to consider some or all of the following decorating ideas for transforming your backdrop into a scene right out of *Sense & Sensibility*.

- Hang the tussie-mussie favors from the guests' chair backs *(see project, page 60)*.
- Place white lace or paper doilies beneath the serving dishes and floral arrangements on the brunch and gift tables.
- Use a blue, white and gold or silver color scheme to go along with the shower theme.

- Serve the food in silver serving dishes, and use formal china. Combine various styles of china to enhance the eclectic feel of the shower.
- Place romantic quotes in gold or silver frames around the room. (Visit www.erasofelegance.com for romantic quotes from the Victorian era.)
- Place arrangements of fresh or dried flowers generously around the party area.

Gift Ideas

Before the bride opens her gifts, present her with the symbolism behind the well-known poem that is the theme of this shower. "Something old" signifies a sense of tradition and represents the link to the bride's old life and her family. Therefore, it would be most appropriate for the bride's mother, grandmother or sister to present this gift.

"Something new" signifies the couple's new beginning and life together as well as their hope for the future. Ask a member of the bride's new family to give the first of the "new" gifts.

For the "something borrowed" part of the phrase, ask a happily married family member or friend to lend something to the bride to wear

or use on her wedding day, such as jewelry or a handkerchief. This signifies the person's wish that the bride's married life will mirror the happiness in her own marriage.

"Something blue" represents fidelity, love and prosperity for the married couple. A close friend or the maid of honor could offer this gift.

Traditionally, we only hear these first four lines mentioned, but the poem is actually finished off with the phrase, "and a sixpence in the shoe." A coin of some kind could be presented to the bride to guarantee prosperity for the couple.

menu

Impress your guests with an elegant brunch that only looks as though it was difficult to prepare. Save yourself some time the day of the shower and prepare the crepes up to a week ahead of time, freezing them until the shower. When it's time to eat, just reheat and serve.

- Crepes with ham and cheese filling and/or berry filling
- Hash Browned Potatoes (see recipe below)
- Lemon Daffodil Cake (see recipe below)
- Fresh orange juice

RECIPES

Hash Browned Potatoes

SERVES 8–10

5 cups Yukon Gold potatoes, peeled and diced

1½ tablespoons clarified butter (see tip below)

1 cup chopped white onion

1 tablespoon chopped fresh chives

1 tablespoon chopped red pepper

Salt and pepper to taste

1. Cook the potatoes in boiling water for 10 minutes or until tender. Remove from heat, drain and set aside.

2. Heat a large skillet over medium heat. Add butter, onions, chives and red pepper and sauté until tender. Add potatoes, salt and pepper. Cook potatoes until they are browned on all sides. Remove from heat and serve.

Lemon Daffodil Cake

SERVES 10–12

White Batter

6 egg whites

1 teaspoon cream of tartar

½ cup sifted cake flour

¾ cup sugar

dash of salt

1. Preheat oven to 350° (177°C).

2. Beat egg whites until foamy. Add cream of tartar. Beat until egg whites form stiff peaks.

3. Sift flour with sugar and salt and fold into egg whites with wire whisk. Pour into tube pan.

Yellow Batter

6 egg yolks

½ cup sugar

½ cup sifted cake flour

1 teaspoon baking powder

dash of salt

3 tablespoons cold water

1. Beat egg yolks, then mix in sugar.

2. Sift flour with baking powder and salt.

3. Add water, 1 tablespoon at a time, alternating with one-third of the flour mixture until all of each is mixed into batter.

4. Pour yellow batter over white batter in pan. If playing the ribbon charm pull game (see page 59), add charms to batter at this stage. Cover charms with about 2" (5cm) of yellow batter. Set the tube pan on a baking sheet and place in oven for 40 minutes or until golden brown.

6. Cover with lemon glaze while still warm.

Lemon Glaze

COVERS 1 CAKE

3¾ cups powdered sugar

¼ cup unsalted butter, room temperature

¼ cup fresh lemon juice

1. Cream sugar and butter together. Mix in juice. Spread over warm Lemon Daffodil Cake.

Tip

Butter is made up of butterfat, milk proteins and water. When butter is clarified, it separates into three layers— the milk proteins and the water are discarded, leaving pure butterfat. To clarify butter, place butter in a pan over very low heat. After the butter separates, gently skim off the foam that rises to the top and discard. Carefully pour the middle layer (butterfat) into a separate container, and discard the milk proteins remaining at the bottom of the pan. Refrigerate any extra clarified butter for later use.

Use only unsalted butter. Clarified butter is used when cooking at high heat where regular butter would burn.

entertainment

The Victorian charm of this shower continues as your guests participate in the activities you have planned. The Lemon Daffodil Cake becomes even more special when you add the custom of ribbon pulls. And your guests can test their knowledge in the Language of Flowers game. These activities may be carried out at the table everyone was eating at, once the brunch food and plates have been cleared.

ribbon charm pull game

The tradition of ribbon pulling dates back to the Victorian era when brides had charms hidden inside their wedding cakes. Each of the bridesmaids would pull a charm out of the cake to discover her fortune. Today the custom of ribbon pulling has become a popular activity for engagement parties, bridal showers and even wedding receptions.

Depending on how many guests are invited, charms could be given to each guest. Cake pulls come in sets of 6, 8, 12 or 18 *(see Resources, page 94)* or you could come up with your own charms. Each charm pull has a different fortune for the individual who pulls it out.

Have the charm pulls baked into the Lemon Daffodil Cake (you may have to make two cakes if you use more than eight charms), or bake into individual cakes or muffins for each guest. One at a time, have each participating guest choose a ribbon to pull from the cake. Announce their fortunes after they pull the charms. Following are some traditional charms and their meanings.

Charm	Meaning	Charm	Meaning	Charm	Meaning
Heart	*true love*	Flower	*blossoming love*	Wreath	*happy home*
Ring	*next engagement*	Anchor	*traveling and adventure*	Rocking chair	*longevity*
Four-leaf clover	*good luck*	High chair	*blessed with children*		

the language of flowers game

People of the Victorian age were often familiar with the meanings associated with various types of flowers. When putting together an arrangement, individuals had to be careful in selecting flowers that might convey a meaning they did not wish to communicate to the recipient.

For this shower game, type a list of the flowers in one column and the meanings, in random order, in a second column. Have the guests match the letter or number next to the meanings with the flower with which it is associated. The guest with the most correct matches wins a prize.

This game could be tied in with the tussie-mussie decoration *(see page 60)* by creating individual bouquets for each guest that feature one of the flowers from the game.

Flower	Meaning
Bluebell	*constancy*
Camellia, white	*perfected loveliness*
Daffodil	*regard*
Daisy	*innocence, newborn*
Forget-Me-Not	*true love*
Gardenia	*ecstasy*
Iris	*faith, wisdom, valor*
Ivy	*fidelity*
Lavender	*luck, devotion*
Lily	*purity, modesty*
Pansy	*loving thoughts*
Periwinkle	*happy memory*
Rose, red	*love*
Rose, white	*charm and innocence*
Rose, white & red	*unity*
Rose, pink	*grace and beauty*
Rose, yellow	*friendship*
Stephanotis	*marital happiness*
Violet, blue	*faithfulness*

tussie-mussie favor

Hang this Victorian tussie-mussie on the back of each person's chair to double as a place marker as well as a party favor.

MATERIALS

2 sheets 12" × 12" (30cm × 30cm) blue/green roses paper

blue cardstock

cream-colored cardstock

Victorian cartouche stamp (Anna Griffin, All Night Media)

paper lace trim (available in the cake decorating section of your craft store)

18" (46cm) of ¾" (19mm) blue satin ribbon

6" (15cm) of ¼" (6mm) blue satin ribbon

artificial white rose, or other flower from The Language of Flowers game *(see page 59)*

artificial blue baby's breath

small piece of floral foam

blue ink pad

blue pen

craft glue

hot glue gun and glue sticks

glue stick

spray adhesive

hole punch

scissors

paring knife

tussie-mussie cone pattern, page 61

1. Mount the two pieces of blue/green roses paper back-to-back using spray adhesive. Smooth out any bubbles. Using the template on page 61, cut a cone out of the double-backed paper. Roll into a cone shape and glue closed with craft glue. The edges at the top should be flush.

2. Measure a length of the paper lace trim to fit around the top of the cone. Begin at one end and fold the lace over the edge of the cone. After folding the paper all the way around, remove it and apply glue with a glue stick on the area of the lace that folds to the inside. Then, beginning at the seam of the cone, adhere the lace to the cone perimeter.

3. Use a knife to trim a piece of floral foam to fit in the cone, tapering it at the end. Glue the foam into the cone with hot glue.

4. Punch two holes at opposite sides of the cone. Thread the ¾" (19mm) ribbon from the inside of the cone through one hole to the outside and tie a knot. Repeat with the other end of the ribbon on the opposite side.

5. Make an arrangement with the flowers and insert it into the foam.

6. Stamp the cartouche onto the cream cardstock, using the blue ink pad. With scissors, cut out the shape, leaving a 1/16" (2mm) border. Glue the cartouche cutout to a piece of blue paper and trim again, leaving about an 1/8" (3mm) border of blue. Leave a larger border at the top of the cartouche to have enough room for a hole to be punched.

7. Using the blue pen, write the name of the guest in the center of the cartouche. Punch a hole in the top of the tag and attach to the lace with a piece of ¼" (6mm) ribbon.

serving tray keepsake

Capture the memories of the bride's and groom's engagement or wedding by creating a unique serving tray they can use for special occasions.

MATERIALS

11" × 14" (28cm × 36cm) gold frame

2 sheets of 12" × 12" (30cm × 30cm) scrapbook paper

white cardstock

bride and groom's wedding announcement

photo of the bride and groom

medium-sized paper doily

pressed flowers

2 metal drawer pulls

4 small nails

white paint

spray glue adhesive

hot glue gun and glue sticks

scissors

paintbrush

steel wool

1. Paint the gold frame white, then distress with steel wool.

2. Hot glue the head of a small nail in each side of the drawer pulls. Lightly hammer the drawer pulls into each short side of the frame.

3. Using the spray adhesive, cover the cardboard insert in the frame with scrapbook paper, aligning the two sheets so the patterns match.

4. Print a favorite quote about love or marriage on a piece of white cardstock. Cut out in a circle to the size of the center of the paper doily and mount on the doily.

5. Place the invitation, photo and doily where you want them in the frame and mount with the spray adhesive.

6. Mount the pressed flowers using a light spray of the adhesive. Replace the cardboard and glass into the frame.

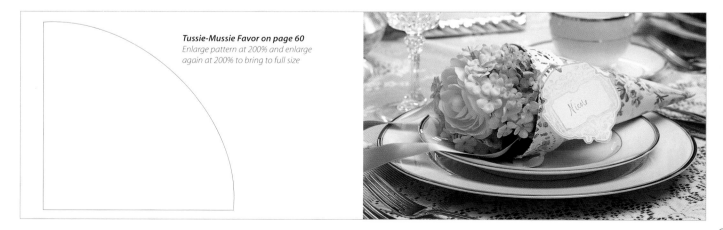

Tussie-Mussie Favor on page 60
Enlarge pattern at 200% and enlarge again at 200% to bring to full size

Fresh Laundry

In the past, it was customary for a bride to be given a trousseau of fine linens in preparation for marriage. Today a woman preparing for marriage needs these same items for her new home, and a laundry-and-linens shower theme gives the bride an opportunity to fine-tune her wish list to items that she really needs or wants. Practical and simple, this shower is filled with bright and cheerful details like laundry bag favors, a delightful towel "cake" and, best of all, an abundance of daisies and good friends.

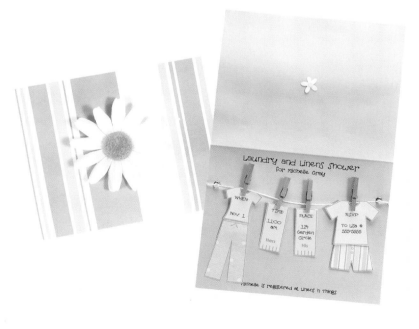

clothesline invitation

The simple charm of this invitation will brighten the day of everyone who opens it. You can almost smell the fresh laundry on the line.

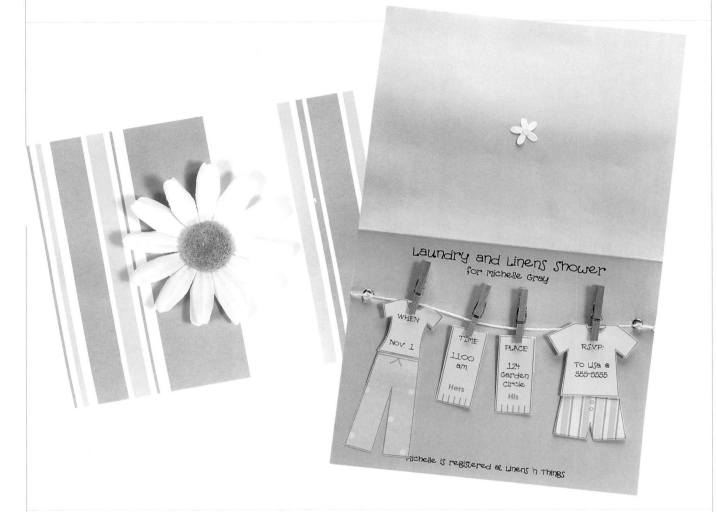

MATERIALS

MATERIALS

12" × 12" (30cm × 30cm) blue double-sided cardstock (striped on one side and solid on the other)

8½" × 11" (22cm × 28cm) white cardstock

patterned scrapbook paper

mini clothesline and clothespins

(see Resources, page 94)

artificial daisy bloom

metal eyelets

mini dimensional adhesive dots

eyelet setter, hammer and mat

scissors

invitation and banner patterns, page 68

1. Cut a piece of double-sided cardstock to 8½" × 11" (22cm × 28cm) and print the invitation wording on the bottom half of the solid side. (You will be able to get two 8⅝" × 5⅜" [22cm × 14cm] cards from this piece of paper.)

2. Print the rest of the invitation wording on white cardstock. Trace the shirt and towel patterns onto the white cardstock, centering each on the words. Trace the pants and shorts patterns onto patterned paper. Cut out each piece.

3. Cut the cardstock down to 8⅝" × 5⅜" (22cm × 14cm), making sure to keep the printed text centered on the card.

4. Fold the card in half lengthwise and glue a daisy on the front.

5. Open the card and insert a metal eyelet on either side of the card *(See Setting Eyelets, page 11)*. Thread the mini clothesline through each side, securing with a double knot.

6. Hang the shirts and towel cutouts from mini clothespins on the clothesline. Adhere the pants and shorts to the card with adhesive dots. If you like, make a small flower from cardstock and glue it to the inside top of the invitation.

decorations

When thinking about laundry and linens, images of bright white, fresh daisies and yellow lemons come to mind, all of which can be incorporated into the decorations for this shower. Here are some ideas for creating a bright and fresh atmosphere.

- Hang a clothesline on a wall or over the serving area. Hang paper cutouts of clothes with clothespins and spell out the bride's and groom's names on the cutouts *(see project below)*.
- Cover the table with a white linen tablecloth or with ticking fabric to match the party favors.
- Serve all of the food on white dishes.
- Use freshly cut daisies and lemons to adorn the serving dishes and table.

- Place arrangements of white daisies around the room. If you have clear vases, fill the bottom with sliced lemons pressed against the sides of the vase before filling with white daisies.
- Wrap the silverware and napkins with a ribbon and daisy, then place the bundles in a small laundry basket on the table.
- Place the laundry bag sachet party favors in a large laundry basket.

hanging clothesline

Pull the linen theme of the shower together in a bright and fresh way with this breezy banner. You can hang it above the gift table to complement the sweet towel cake (page 69), or string it up above the No-Bake Lemon Cheesecake (page 68) to make your serving table even more appealing.

Enlarge the clothing patterns on page 68, then trace them onto solid or patterned cardstock and cut out.

Print the bride's and groom's names on the bottoms of two pieces of cardstock and cut the paper down to 4½" (11cm) wide for the "towels." Hot glue a daisy bloom in the middle of each towel and make small cuts at each end to create fringe. Hang the towels and clothing from a clothesline with wooden clothespins, then hot glue a daisy bloom on either end of the clothesline.

entertainment

This shower is the perfect opportunity to play some fun games, each with a laundry theme. In the first game, the guests' knowledge of the couple will be put "on the line," and the second game will test their laundry know-how. To reward the winners of each game, give them laundry sachets for their linen closets or clothing drawers.

love on the line

Prepare questions about the bride and groom's courtship for the guests to answer at the shower. Write the questions on clothes-, towel- or other linen-shaped paper cutouts and hang from a clothesline. Have each guest choose one of the questions to read aloud. Each person should have a sheet of paper and a pen or pencil to write down the answer to each question. The person who correctly answers the most questions wins a prize. Here are some sample questions to get you started:

How did the bride and groom meet?
What did the bride and groom do on their first date?
How did the groom propose?
What does _____ say is the most romantic thing he has ever done for her?
What personality trait does the bride like best about her fiancé?
Where will the couple be spending their honeymoon?

laundry basket pricing game

Fill a laundry basket with a variety of laundry items. Have each guest guess the total cost of all the items. The person with the closest guess wins a prize and the laundry basket of supplies goes to the bride. You could fill the basket with any or all of the following items:

Laundry detergent   Bleach
Stain remover   Woolite
Dryer sheets   Spray bottle
Fabric softener   Borax detergent
Starch spray

mini laundry bag favor

What a perfect gift to give your shower guests as they head home! Fill this miniature laundry bag with candy, soaps or small laundry cleaning items to help them remember this special event.

Tip

To make sure the cording feeds smoothly into the channel, sew the side seams of the bag flat so the cording will not catch any loose material.

1. Make the First Seam

Cut out a 6" × 24" (15cm × 61cm) piece of yellow ticking fabric and fold in half widthwise, with the right sides together. Sew the sides of the bag with a ⅜" (10mm) seam. Iron the seams open.

2. Fold Down Top

Fold over a ⅜" (10mm) seam on the open end of the bag and iron flat. Sew the seam.

3. Fold Over Again

Fold the top over another 3¼" (8cm), which includes the first folded-down seam, and iron flat.

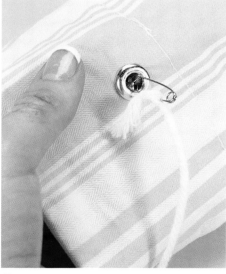

4. Make Mark for Grommet

Turn the bag right side out and mark the spot where the grommet will be placed, about 2½" (6cm) from the top fold.

5. Add the Grommet and Cord

With the grommet tool, punch a hole through one layer of the material only, not the layer that is folded down. Push the top half of the grommet through the hole, then slide the bottom half of the grommet underneath and press together with the tool *(see Setting Grommets, page 11)*. Turn the bag inside out again and sew along the seam of the first fold to make a channel for the cording. Be careful not to sew through to the other side of the bag. Turn the bag right side out. Attach a small safety pin to the piece of cording and feed through the grommet.

6. Add the Candy and Daisy

Work the safety pin and cording around the bag and back out of the grommet. Fill the cellophane bag with the favor item and place in the laundry bag. Tie the cording into a bow and knot each end. Hot glue the daisy bloom just below the bow on the bag, trimming the stem short first.

menu

The menu for this fresh-themed shower is as light and refreshing as a breeze through the backyard. Everything about this shower, including the food, is meant to be simple, fresh and light. A serve-yourself salad bar allows your guests to create a meal to fit their tastes without creating more work for you.

- Build-your-own chef salads
- Fresh fruit and fruit dip *(see recipe below)*
- No-Bake Lemon Cheesecake *(see recipe below)*
- Fresh lemonade

RECIPES

Fruit Dip
SERVES 10

1 8-ounce package cream cheese

1 7-ounce jar marshmallow cream

1 tablespoon lemon juice

1. Mix all of the ingredients together and chill until ready to serve. Serve with fresh cut apples, strawberries, pears and grapes.

No-Bake Lemon Cheesecake
SERVES 8

Filling:

1 cup water

1 small package lemon gelatin

1 large can evaporated milk, chilled

2 tablespoons lemon juice

½ cup sugar

1 8-ounce package cream cheese, softened

Crust:

2 cups finely crushed animal crackers

½ cup butter, melted

2 tablespoons sugar

1. For filling, bring water to a boil in a saucepan. Add gelatin and mix. Allow mixture to cool in refrigerator.

2. With a hand mixer, whip the chilled evaporated milk to a cream-like consistency and add lemon juice. Whip until stiff peaks form. Fold in sugar.

3. Place the cream cheese in a separate mixing bowl and add 1 cup of the whipped mixture. Add the remaining whipped mixture and beat until smooth; add in cooled gelatin.

4. Mix crust ingredients and spread ⅔ of the mixture in the bottom and sides of a pie pan. Pour filling on top of crust. Place remaining crust mixture on top of cheesecake. Chill until ready to serve.

5. Garnish with freshly cut lemon slices. Cut the lemon slices to the center and twist to sit on top of each slice of cheesecake.

Invitation Clothing and Banner Clothing on pages 64 and 65
For invitation, reduce patterns by 70%. For banner, enlarge patterns at 200%, enlarge again at 200%, and enlarge again at 139% to bring to full size

towel cake gift

Since the gift options for this shower are narrowed to linens and laundry supplies, you may want to allow the guests to contribute money for the bride to buy something special she needs for her new home. A cute way to present the bride with this money is with a towel cake.

Use a white bath towel, hand towel and washcloth to make a three-tiered "wedding cake." Decorate the cake with ribbon and daisies. Have each guest who is contributing money fold up the bills and slide them into the towel rolls of the cake. Attach a card to the cake with signatures of all those who contributed.

MATERIALS

1 white bath towel
1 white hand towel
1 white washcloth
90" (2m) yellow gingham ribbon
9 yellow silk daisies, stems trimmed off
straight pins
corsage pins

1. Fold the bath towel in half, lengthwise.

2. Fold the towel again, in thirds, lengthwise.

3. Loosely roll the towel, keeping the edges straight.

4. Secure the towel roll with corsage pins. Set aside.

5. Fold the hand towel and the washcloth into thirds and roll up. Secure in the back with corsage pins.

6. Stack the towel layers in the form of a cake. Wrap a length of ribbon around the bottom layer and secure in the front with straight pins.

7. Create a bow by tying two loops into a knot.

8. Pull the bow snugly and then bring one of the tails over the top of the knot.

9. Secure the bow to the center of the ribbon band around the towel with a corsage pin. Repeat the ribbon bands and bows for the other two layers of the cake. Arrange daisy blooms evenly around the cake.

10. Secure the flowers to the towels by placing straight pins under the top layer of petals.

To Everything a Season

After the wedding, the bride and groom will have the opportunity to start time-honored traditions within their new family. Whether it's using a special plate for birthday cake or sharing favorite stories of the past year on New Year's Eve, these traditions make each family unique. This shower celebrates the seasons that are so closely tied to family traditions. Each guest brings a gift that relates to one season of the year, and she shares a tradition that her family observes during that same season.

As the bride-to-be passes from single to married life, she'll have lasting memories of this timeless shower and of the guests who helped her create new family traditions.

seasons invitation

The simple sophistication of this petal-shaped invitation beautifully communicates the season theme for this shower. The green linen paper used here and for the favor boxes adds to the elegance.

MATERIALS

12" × 12" (30cm × 30cm) green linen cardstock

off-white cardstock

leaf print handmade paper

9 metal eyelets

28" (71cm) of ⅛" (3mm) green satin ribbon

brass seasons stencil (All Night Media)

glue stick

eyelet setter, hammer and mat

⅛" (3mm) hole punch

bone folder

stylus

scissors

petal envelope pattern, page 77

Tip

To dry emboss paper, tape the brass stencil to the paper the way you'd like the image to appear. Place the stencil side on a light box or a sunny window. With the stylus, apply pressure to the paper and trace all parts of the stencil image. Remove the tape and the stencil to reveal the embossed image.

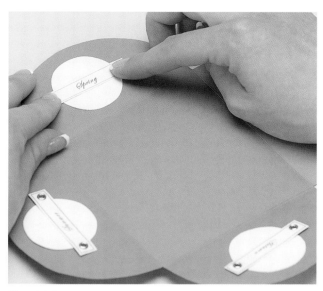

1. Mount the Circles

Using the template on page 77, cut out a petal-shaped envelope from a piece of green linen cardstock. Score the lines for each of the four folds. Use the seasons stencil to dry emboss four different cardstock circles and glue one in the center of each petal.

2. Add the Seasons Strips

Print the names of each season on off-white cardstock and cut into small strips. Punch holes on each short end of the paper strips, then set eyelets in each hole *(see Setting Eyelets, page 11)*. Glue the strips across the embossed circles.

3. Add the Invitation Wording

Print the wording for the invitation on a 4" × 4" (10cm × 10cm) piece of off-white cardstock and cover with a 4" × 4" (10cm × 10cm) piece of the handmade paper. Hold the two pieces together and punch two holes near the top of the paper, spacing the holes 1" (3cm) apart. Thread 12" (31cm) of the ribbon through the holes and tie a bow to hold the two pieces of paper together.

4. Fold the Envelope Flaps

Fold the flaps on the scored lines. Place the pieces from step 3 in the center of the envelope. Fold one flap over the other to close the envelope.

5. Secure With a Ribbon

Print a 1¾" (5cm) circle with the words, "To everything there is a season, and a time for every purpose" onto a piece of off-white cardstock and cut out. Set an eyelet in the center of the circle. Wrap 15" (38cm) of green ribbon around the envelope and bring both ends through the back of the eyelet to the front. Tie a knot to secure.

wedding wreath keepsake

Like a traditional Advent calendar, this Wedding Wreath helps the bride- and groom-to-be count down the days to their special event. Each day before the wedding, the couple opens one of the envelopes on the wreath to find a note or bit of advice from one of the guests at the shower.

Before the shower, purchase a pre-made wreath for the base. Punch a hole in the top of each small envelope *(see pattern, page 77)*, one for each attendee at the shower. Prepare small cards to fit inside the envelopes, printing a love quote on one side of each card, if you like. Cut small circles out of off-white cardstock and stamp with a number from one to fourteen (or how ever many envelopes you choose to attach to the wreath). Punch a small hole in the top of each numbered circle and thread a piece of ribbon through the hole, leaving the ends untied.

At the shower, as the guests arrive, have them write a short message on the back of one of the cards and place it in one of the envelopes that will be attached to the wreath. Attach a number to each envelope and tie each envelope to the wreath.

As the couple opens the envelopes they may choose to return the cards and envelopes to the wreath, or create their own envelopes for holidays throughout the year. Either way, the wreath will make a beautiful decoration for their home.

napkin rings favor

Give each guest the opportunity to create her own set of seasonal napkin rings during the shower. Provide them with a pillow box (that you've made ahead of time) to place their napkin rings in when finished.

MATERIALS

12" × 12" (30cm × 30cm) green linen cardstock

small piece of off-white cardstock

piece of handmade paper

⅛" (3mm) metal eyelet polymer clay in a variety of colors to represent each season

variety of small buttons in seasonal shapes such as snowflakes, ornaments, flowers and leaves

variety of narrow ribbons and raffia

glue stick

brass seasons stencil (All Night Media)

eyelet setter, hammer and mat

⅛" (3mm) hole punch

bone folder

stylus

bamboo skewer

scissors

box favor pattern, page 77

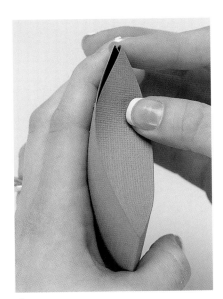

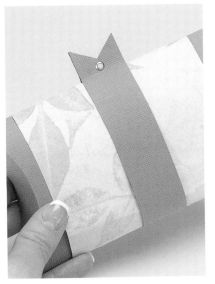

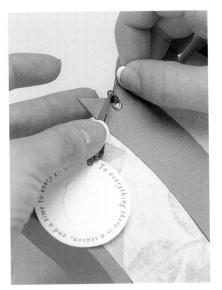

1. Create the Pillow Box

Using the template on page 77, cut a pillow box form from the green linen cardstock. Score on the marked folding lines with a bone folder. Glue the pillow box closed and fold in the sides, following the scored line.

2. Wrap With Paper Ribbon

Cut a 4¼" × 10" (11cm × 25cm) piece from the handmade paper and wrap around the pillow box; glue the paper strip together where it overlaps. Using the template on page 77, cut out a ribbon using the green cardstock. Wrap the paper ribbon around the pillow box and attach at the top with a metal eyelet.

3. Add the Tag

Print a 1¾" (5cm) circle with the words, "To everything there is a season, and a time for every purpose" onto a piece of off-white cardstock and cut out. With a stylus, dry emboss one of the seasonal images in the center of the circle cutout. Punch a hole at the edge of the circle, or set an eyelet, and attach the circle to the paper ribbon with a piece of green ribbon.

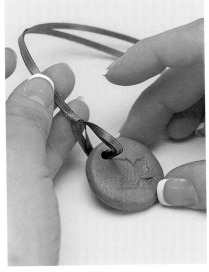

4. Divide the Clay

Cut a section of polymer clay into quarters.

5. Emboss Images Into the Clay

Press a quartered piece of clay into a 1¼" (3cm) circle. Press a button image into the center of the clay. Have the guests repeat this step with each color of clay, using images for each of the four seasons.

6. Tie the Pieces With Ribbon

Use a bamboo skewer to poke a hole in the top center of the clay. Bake at 275° (135°C) for 20 minutes. When cool, thread a ribbon through the hole in the clay piece. The ribbon ties around a napkin to form a napkin ring.

decorations

There are plenty of options for decorating for a seasons shower, but don't go overboard by pulling out all of your seasonal items. Begin with a palette of greens and other earthy colors and add a few decorations to represent each season of the year. Here are some additional decorating suggestions.

- Decorate a small folding table for each season of the year. To keep it simple, use the same basic centerpiece, such as a topiary or wreath, in the middle of each table and add seasonal adornments to each.
- Hang the photos that will be used for the Photo Match game *(see below)* from a ribbon or grapevine suspended between two walls or other anchoring points; make sure it is a space that will easily allow the guests to view the pictures for the game.
- Place the cards for the keepsake wreath *(see project, page 74)* in a basket on a small table by the entrance, allowing space for the guests to write their advice or traditions.

- Separate the serving table into four areas and label each for one of the seasons so guests know where to place their potluck dishes.
- Hang the keepsake wreath above the gift area.
- Create a display of mementos from different seasons of the bride's life. For instance, a pair of baby booties, her favorite blanket or doll from her childhood, pom-poms from high school and the veil for her wedding.

entertainment

The activities at this shower will keep your guests' minds and hands busy. Test their knowledge during the Photo Match game, then let them explore their creativity as they make their own set of Seasonal Napkin Rings *(see page 74)*.

photo match game

See how well your guests really know the bride and groom with this game. Ask the parents of the happy couple for help thinking of important life events for the game. To set up this game, gather five pictures of the bride and five pictures of the groom. The photos should be from a variety of years including a shot of each as a baby, up until the time of their courtship. Mount the photos on the same green cardstock used in the invitation and write or stamp a visible number on each. Hang all of the photos from ribbons suspended from the ceiling or from a grapevine swag.

Provide each guest with a piece of paper on which they will match each photo with a certain event that took place during the year the photo was taken. Have the papers printed ahead of time with phrases such as "This individual broke a leg in 1997." The guest then writes on the paper the number of the photo she believes corresponds with each event. The person who makes the most correct matches wins a prize.

Gift Ideas

Assign each guest one of the four seasons and have her bring a gift appropriate for that season. As the bride opens her gifts, have the person whose gift she is opening tell a favorite family tradition from a holiday during that season. For instance, if the guest brought a gift for the spring season, she could share a favorite Easter tradition. Keep a list of the traditions for the bride to think about incorporating into her new family traditions.

menu

In addition to assigning a season for which they should bring an appropriate gift, ask each guest to bring an appetizer or dessert that goes along with that season as well. As the host, you may want to provide sandwiches and a beverage for this potluck buffet.

- Potluck meal
- Chicken salad sandwiches *(see recipe below)*

- Laurie's Raspberry Lemonade *(see recipe, page 41)*

RECIPES

Chicken Salad
SERVES 20

4 pounds boneless, skinless chicken breasts

2 tablespoons salt

2 teaspoons pepper

¾ cup peeled and diced white onion

¾ cup diced celery

1 cup chopped apple

1½ cups mayonnaise

1. Preheat oven to 350° (177°C).

2. Season the chicken with the salt and pepper. Bake chicken for 35–45 minutes. Refrigerate the chicken for at least an hour, then shred.

3. Mix shredded chicken with remaining ingredients, adding additional salt and pepper to taste. Chill in refrigerator until ready to serve. Serve on croissants or hard rolls.

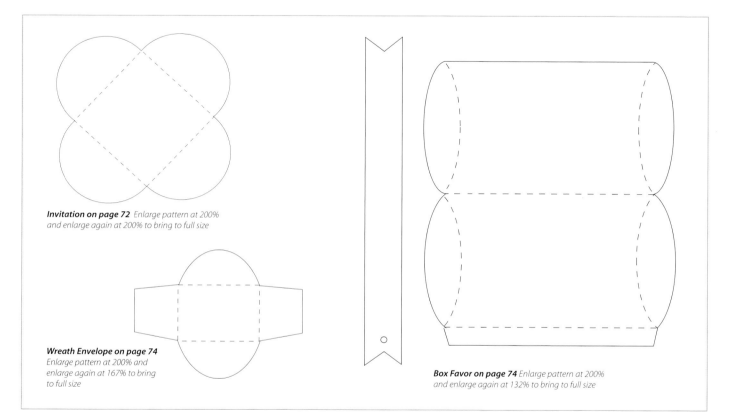

Invitation on page 72 *Enlarge pattern at 200% and enlarge again at 200% to bring to full size*

Wreath Envelope on page 74
Enlarge pattern at 200% and enlarge again at 167% to bring to full size

Box Favor on page 74 *Enlarge pattern at 200% and enlarge again at 132% to bring to full size*

Love is in the Air

A wedding is the most romantic occasion in any person's life, and this bridal shower incorporates many symbols of romance—candles, roses, hearts and, of course, lingerie. Lingerie is a favorite shower gift, and this shower is meant to provide the bride with a great array of lingerie and sleepwear. The shower invitations, which arrive in a miniature lingerie store bag, set the tone. An appetizer and dessert buffet with fondue and heart candle party favors continue the romantic theme. There is no doubt the air will be filled with love as you prepare the blushing bride for her honeymoon night.

lingerie bag invitation

Your guests will be inspired to shop for a shower gift after receiving their invitation inside a mini lingerie shopping bag. To get your guests "in the mood," create your own lingerie-shaped invitation *(as shown at right)* and print the time, date and location of the shower on it. If you don't want to narrow the gift-giving to only lingerie, change the shape of the invitation from lingerie to a heart or other love-inspired shape of your choice.

MATERIALS

12" × 12" (30cm × 30cm) pink rose paper

pink tissue paper

four ¼" (6mm) grommets

black satin cording

glue stick

grommet setting tool

bone folder

scissors

invitation bag pattern, page 85

Gift Ideas

In the invitation to the shower, ask your guests to give gifts of lingerie or other sleepwear—and be sure to include the bride's size. In addition, you could also suggest bath items, perfume or jewelry as other thoughtful gift options.

Have the guests open a fortune cookie and read the love fortune for the bride and groom as the bride is opening the gift they brought.

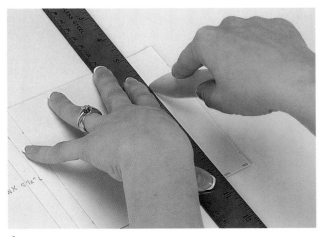

1. Cut Out the Paper

Use the template on page 85 to trace a shopping bag form on the pink rose paper. Score the fold lines with a bone folder.

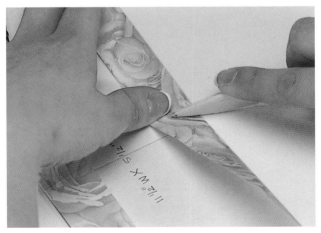

2. Score Where Indicated

Cut out the bag, then use the bone folder to crease the folds.

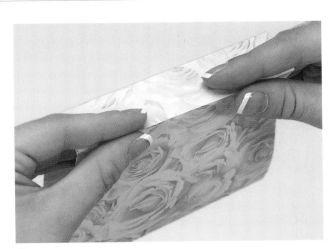

3. Fold Over the Top

Fold over the top edge of the bag.

4. Glue Sides of Bag

Glue the sides together.

5. Fold in the Bottom

Fold in the bottom and glue closed.

6. Mark and Set Grommets

With a pencil, mark the spots for the grommets, placing the marks about ½" (1cm) from the top of the bag and 2½" (6cm) apart. Cut the holes with the grommet tool, then repeat on the other side of the bag. Insert a grommet into each hole and set with the setter tool.

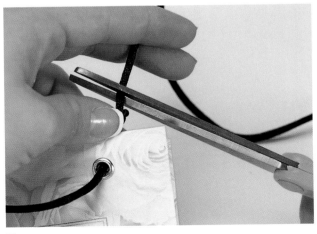

7. Tie on Cording

Thread a 14" (36cm) piece of satin cording through both holes on one side of the bag and secure in the inside of the bag with a knot. Repeat on the other side.

8. Insert Invitation

Wrap invitation in pink tissue paper and insert in bag.

decorations

Every detail of this shower is meant to create a feeling of romance. Help your guests feel as though they've been swept away with this list of decorating ideas.

- Hang the "Love" banner *(see project below)* over the serving area or in another prominent spot.
- Place black-and-white photos of the bride and groom in black frames around the room.
- Place a large arrangement of antique pink roses in the center of the serving table.

- Cover the serving and gift tables with white or pink tablecloths.
- Create displays of white and pink candles of varying sizes around the room.
- Use white dishes for serving the food.
- Arrange a platter of chocolates for your guests to snack on.

love banner
Love will be in the air, literally, when you hang this banner above the serving area, near the gift table, or in any spot at your shower.

To make the banner, cut four sheets of rose-patterned scrapbook paper to 8½" x 11" (22cm x 28cm). Print each sheet with one letter of the word "love," using a large point size for the font. Cut a heart shape around each letter. Glue each heart onto a piece of white cardstock, then cut around the heart, leaving a ⅛" (3mm) border of white. My finished hearts measure 10" x 8½" (25cm x 22cm). Punch a hole and set an eyelet at the top center of each heart, and thread a ¼" (6mm) wide ribbon through each eyelet. Hang the letters by the ribbon.

entertainment

Keep romance in the forefront by playing the Movie and Song Matching Game, which has guests match romantic movies to their theme song. Finally, at the end of the shower, as a romantic surprise for the bride-to-be, ask her groom to arrive with a bouquet of roses. Ask him to tell his fiancée a reason why he loves her for each of the roses in the bouquet.

movie and song matching game

On a sheet of paper, create a list of titles of romantic movies. In a second column, in random order, list the song featured in each movie, accompanied by a letter or number. Make a copy for each guest, and at the shower, ask the players to write down the letter or number of the song that goes with the romantic movie in which it played. Award the guest who gets the most correct with the soundtrack from one of the films on the list. At right is a list of suggested movies and songs.

Movie	Song
Say Anything	*In Your Eyes, Peter Gabriel*
Titanic	*My Heart Will Go On, Celine Dion*
Sleepless in Seattle	*When I Fall in Love, Celine Dion*
Ghost	*Unchained Melody, Righteous Brothers*
The Wedding Planner	*I Can't Help Myself, Nobody's Angel*
The Princess Bride	*Storybook Love, Willy Deville*
Notting Hill	*I Do (Cherish You), 98 Degrees*
Pretty Woman	*It Must Have Been Love, Roxette*
Return to Me	*What If I Loved You, Joey Gian*
The Wedding Singer	*Every Little Thing She Does is Magic, The Police*
Runaway Bride	*I Love You, Martina McBride*
An Officer & A Gentleman	*Up Where We Belong, Joe Cocker*
You've Got Mail	*Dreams, Cranberries*
What Women Want	*Too Marvelous For Words, Frank Sinatra*
Serendipity	*To Remind Me, Brian Whitman*
Bed of Roses	*Ice Cream, Sarah McLachlan*

menu

A tantalizing spread of appetizers and desserts served with fondue is appropriate for this shower. With a little preparation the day before the party, serving a fondue menu will not only be easy, but is sure to be a crowd pleaser with your guests. Wait to serve the fortune cookies to your guests until the bride-to-be opens her gifts *(see Gift Ideas, page 80)*.

- Cheese Fondue
- Chocolate Fondue *(see recipe below)*
- Love Fortune Cookies *(see recipe below)*
- Sparkling Cranberry Punch *(see recipe below)*

RECIPES

Chocolate Fondue

SERVES 6–8

1 cup semi-sweet chocolate pieces

½ cup evaporated milk

¼ cup marshmallows

½ teaspoon vanilla extract

1. Combine all of the ingredients in a heavy saucepan and cook over low heat until smooth. Keep warm in a fondue pan. Serve with marshmallows, strawberries, bananas, angel food cake and brownies.

Love Fortune Cookies

MAKES 24 COOKIES

2 egg whites *(at room temperature)*

½ cup superfine sugar

¼ teaspoon salt

½ teaspoon vanilla extract

1 tablespoon butter

½ cup flour

1. Print love-themed fortunes on thin paper and cut into strips. Preheat oven to 400° (204°C), and grease two large nonstick cookie sheets. Mix all of the ingredients together until well blended.

2. Drop one large tablespoon of dough onto the cookie sheet and spread into a large circle (about 5" [13cm] in diameter) with the back of a spoon. Repeat for one more cookie on that cookie sheet. (You can only bake two cookies at a time because they will get too hard to fold sitting on the pan if there are more than two.) Bake cookies for 5 minutes or until edges are golden brown.

3. Remove one cookie at a time from the sheet with a metal spatula and place the bottom side up on a work surface. Place a quote strip in the center of the cookie. Fold the cookie in half. Then, place the folded edge down on the rim of a bowl or glass to bend in half. Repeat with the rest of the dough.

Sparkling Cranberry Punch

MAKES 12 SERVINGS

2 quarts cranberry juice, chilled

1 can (12 ounces) frozen lemonade concentrate, thawed

1 quart sparkling water, chilled

1. In a large punch bowl, combine the cranberry juice and lemonade concentrate. Stir in the sparkling water and serve.

2. For an added touch, make an ice ring. Add real cranberries or plastic hearts to water in a bundt cake pan and freeze. Float in the punch when ready to serve.

heart candles favor

Let your guests take some of the romance home with them with these pretty heart candles. Wrap them in pink tissue paper and place them in a small rose paper bag, just like the one used for the invitation.

MATERIALS

crystallizing candle wax
red food coloring or red wax shavings
candle fragrance
wicks, cut to 2" (5cm) each
double-boiler
heart-shaped floating candle molds
candle- or candy-making thermometer

1. Following the manufacturer's instructions on the wax package, melt the wax in a double-boiler.

2. When the wax has reached the correct temperature, stir in the coloring or wax shavings, along with three to four drops of candle fragrance.

3. Fill the molds two-thirds full with the melted wax and allow to cool for about 10–15 minutes. (Return the left over wax to the stove on low heat.)

4. Place a wick in the center of each candle, pressing down just a little.

5. Reheat the left over wax to the proper temperature and pour into the molds to fill to the top.

6. Allow the candles to cool for 30 minutes or more and remove from the molds.

romantic advice keepsake

Help the bride- and groom-to-be have a lifetime of romance with advice from the shower guests. Ask each guest to write down a tip for keeping the romance alive in their marriage. Have paper hearts made for the guests to write on, and place the cards in a keepsake jar for the couple. The cards pictured here are made with printed rose paper. A piece of vellum paper is attached to the patterned paper with a heart eyelet.

Tip

For another keepsake gift, use the roses from the groom (see page 82) to create an heirloom rose box.

Dry the roses that the groom-to-be gives his fiancée by hanging them upside down in a dark, cool place. Glue the roses, or just the rose heads, in a shadow box. Place the roses so that they surround a card that lists all of the reasons the groom gave for why he loves his bride-to-be (one for each rose).

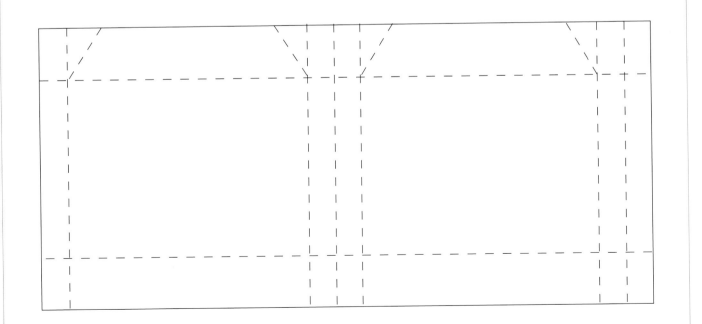

Lingerie Bag on pages 80 and 84 *Enlarge pattern at 182% to bring to full size*

Paradise Luau

Create a tropical paradise in which the wedding couple and their friends escape for an evening celebration.

Traditionally held outdoors at sunset, a luau shower offers a romantic setting for the bride and groom to get a small preview of a more extended honeymoon getaway. This party is a perfect opportunity for the wedding couple to become acquainted with each other's friends because it can accommodate a large guest list that includes both couples and singles. Get ready for an evening in paradise.

Hawaiian invitation

Prepare your guests for an evening of fun in paradise with this vibrant invitation. The Hawaiian patterned paper and island flowers will get everyone in the mood for a luau.

Aloha

COME CELEBRATE THE UPCOMING MARRIAGE OF
JON AND KELLY
AT THEIR WEDDING SHOWER LUAU.
PLEASE DRESS IN YOUR HAWAIIAN BEST!

WHEN: SATURDAY, JUNE 14TH
TIME: 6:00 P.M.
WHERE: 580 N. COLUMBIA AVE.
R.S.V.P.: BY JUNE 10TH

JON AND KELLY ARE REGISTERED AT:
LINENS N THINGS, CRATE & BARREL and TARGET

MATERIALS

12" × 12" (30cm × 30cm) green Hawaiian patterned paper

bright pink, yellow, green and orange cardstock

rice paper

white square envelope, 5" × 5" (13cm × 13cm)

raffia

thin bamboo or sugar cane, dried

⅛" (3mm) eyelets in bright colors

glue stick

hot glue gun and glue sticks

craft knife

bone folder

scissors

⅛" (3mm) hole punch

eyelet setter, hammer and mat

invitation flower patterns, page 93

Gift Ideas

This shower, a gathering of both the bride's and groom's friends, is a great opportunity to have some fun with the gifts. Assign the guys to bring a gift for the bride and the ladies to bring a gift for the groom.

1. Fold the Patterned Paper

Cut a piece of patterned paper to 9¼" × 4⅝" (23cm × 12cm). With the pattern side facing up, fold short sides to meet in the center. Crease with a bone folder.

2. Add the Wording

Design the wording for the invitation on a computer (see Resources, page 94 for fonts). Cut a piece of rice paper to 8½" × 11" (22cm× 28cm) and attach it to a piece of regular paper with a small piece of tape on either side. Print the wording on the rice paper, and trim down to 4⅛" × 4⅛" (11cm × 11cm). Glue just the top of the rice paper square in the center of the card with a glue stick. Cut a piece of bamboo or sugar cane to 4" (10cm) and attach it to the top of the rice paper with a strip of hot glue.

3. Add the Small Flower

Cut a small flower shape using the pattern on page 93 from any color cardstock (pictured here in green). Glue the flower on a piece of contrasting cardstock (shown above in bright pink) and trim around the flower leaving a ⅛" (3mm) border around the edges. Punch a hole in the center of the layered flower, and set an eyelet (see Setting Eyelets, page 11). Glue the flower to the bottom left corner of the rice paper. Feel free to experiment with different color combinations on each invitation.

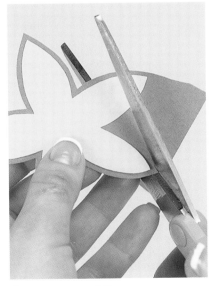

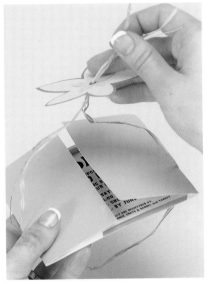

4. Create Second Flower

Using the medium pattern on page 93, cut out a hibiscus flower in any color cardstock for the front of the invitation. Glue it to a piece of contrasting cardstock and cut out, leaving a border of ⅛" (3mm).

5. Wrap Card with Raffia

Cut a small flower from any color of cardstock (shown here in orange) and attach to the medium flower with the border (pictured above in yellow and pink) with an eyelet. Cut a 12" (30cm) length of raffia and thread both ends through the eyelet in the middle of the flower. Slide the card through the raffia loop.

6. Secure with a Knot

Pull the raffia snugly, then knot to secure. Add a small layered flower to the back of the envelope with an eyelet.

decorations

To give your luau an authentic feel, use natural items, such as tropical flowers, plants and fruit to create an island paradise setting for your guests. Since food is a major component of any luau, be sure to make your serving area the focus of the party through the decorations you choose. Consider some or all of the following suggestions to prepare your setting in paradise.

- Cover your table with a white tablecloth and bamboo table runner.
- Arrange artificial ti leaves (green, spiky tropical leaves native to Hawaii and often used to make leis) beneath the serving dishes on the table.
- Place papayas and mangoes, cut in half lengthwise, around the serving dishes.
- Place real pineapples and coconuts on the serving table.
- Line the path to the party entrance and the party area with tiki torches. If it is not possible to stick the torches into the ground, fill galvanized buckets with sand to hold the torches up.
- Use a generous amount of tropical flowers, real or fake, in arrangements on the eating tables and individually scattered around the serving area.
- Serve the food in rustic baskets or wooden bowls.

- Set potted palm trees or hibiscus plants around the party setting.
- Add lanterns and candles for ambience. If there is a pool or other water feature in the party area, place floating candles there for a nice touch.
- Create centerpieces for the tables by setting a candle hurricane in the middle of a rattan charger, then surround with hibiscus flowers. Wrap the glass with rice paper and glue to secure. Make flowers as you did for the invitation and tie them with raffia around the candle *(see photo, page 91)*.
- Make a sign that says "Love in Paradise" and set in the center of the serving area *(see project below)*.
- Have Hawaiian music playing in the background.
- Give your guests a traditional Hawaiian welcome by placing leis around their necks as they arrive.

love in paradise sign
Create this sign for a fun and clever way to announce your theme. It uses the same paper as the invitations on page 88.

MATERIALS

12" × 12" (30cm × 30cm) green patterned paper

8½" × 11"(22cm × 28cm) white text paper

thin bamboo or sugar cane, dried

3 bamboo sticks, cut to between 20" and 30" (51cm and 76cm)

raffia

⅛" (3mm) eyelets

3 coconut halves, dried

glue stick

hot glue gun and glue sticks

⅛" (3mm) hole punch

eyelet setter, hammer and mat

scissors

hand drill

banner pattern, page 93

1. Use the pattern on page 93 to create the flowers from Hawaiian patterned paper. Print one word on a sheet of white paper, cut into a smaller flower shape and glue to the patterned flower.

2. Punch a hole in the top center of each flower and set an eyelet in each hole. Thread raffia up through the hole, wrap a piece of bamboo around the raffia, then thread the raffia back down through the hole. Tie the raffia into a knot at the back on the flower to secure the bamboo.

3. Tie another knot 1" (3cm) down the raffia to create a loop. Tie additional raffia beneath the loop at the back, and allow this raffia to hang down.

4. Drill a hole in each of the coconut halves, making the holes large enough for one of the bamboo sticks to be inserted.

5. Place the loop on the back of each flower over one end of each bamboo stick. Place the other end of each stick into a coconut.

menu

The food served at this shower is really part of the entertainment. While serving a traditional luau might seem a little overwhelming, it is actually quite easy. Most of the items on the menu can be purchased pre-made from a supermarket, leaving you with just a few dishes to prepare.

- Cocktail shrimp, served in an ice bowl, with tropical flowers frozen inside
- Oven Roasted Pork *(see recipe below)*
- Rice or baked sweet potatoes
- Fruit kabobs: Strawberry, pineapple, grape and banana pieces on a wooden skewer

- Hawaiian macaroni salad
- Macadamia nuts
- Hawaiian sweet bread
- Honeymoon "Passion" Punch *(see recipe below)*

RECIPES

Honeymoon "Passion" Punch
SERVES 16

4 cups pineapple juice

4 cups passion fruit juice

4 cups Hawaiian fruit punch

4 cups lemon-lime soda

1. Mix first two ingredients and chill.

2. Freeze fruit punch into heart-shape ice cubes.

3. Add soda and ice cubes to punch just before serving.

Oven Roasted Pork
SERVES 8

4 pounds pork butt roast

¼ cup liquid smoke

2 tablespoons rock salt

soy sauce *(according to taste)*

2 tablespoons olive oil

10-ounce package frozen spinach, chopped, thawed and drained

1 white onion, diced

1. Preheat oven to 550° (288°C). Cut ¼" (6mm) deep slits about 1" (3 cm) apart on each side of the roast. Rub rock salt and liquid smoke all over the roast, working both into the slits. Wrap the roast tightly in aluminum foil and let sit for 30 minutes.

2. Cook roast for 45 minutes. Lower heat to 400° (204°C) and cook roast for three more hours, or until tender. Shred the pork and remove any fat.

3. Sauté the diced onion in olive oil over medium heat for about two minutes or until tender. Add the spinach and sauté until heated through. Combine the sautéed onions and spinach with the shredded pork and soy sauce. Serve over rice or with sweet potatoes.

entertainment

Two necessities for any luau: Hawaiian music and leis. Set the stage for your luau by having Hawaiian music playing in the background, then greet your guests in the traditional Hawaiian way—with a lei that they'll use for the Hawaiian Word Game.

Rachel
(Leikela)
Kuaua: Shower

JOEL
(Ioela)
Male'ana : Wedding

Sharon
(Kalona)
Male: Married Man

Hawaiian word game

Greet guests as they arrive with a lei that has their name and a Hawaiian word having to do with love or marriage printed on a tag that's attached to it (be sure to give the bride and groom a more elaborate lei). The English translation for the word will be printed next to or under the Hawaiian word. Give the guests a list of all the Hawaiian words and 10 to15 minutes at the beginning of the shower to mingle with one another and write down the English meaning next to the Hawaiian words listed on their paper. The person with the most correct translations at the end of the time wins a prize.

MATERIALS

8½" × 11" (22cm × 28cm)
white cardstock

colored cardstock

artificial flower leis (available at party stores)

flower stickers

raffia

⅛" (3mm) eyelets

glue stick

⅛" (3mm) hole punch

eyelet setter, hammer and mat

scissors

name tag pattern, page 93

1. Print each guest's name and a Hawaiian word *(see the list at right for word suggestions)* on the computer (here I included a Hawaiian name for each guest as well). Cut the name tag into a flower shape using the pattern on page 93.

2. Mount the name tag onto colored cardstock and cut out to make a border.

3. Punch a hole at the top of the flower and set an eyelet. Attach the flower to the lei with a raffia tie. Add flower stickers to the name tag, if desired.

Hawaiian Word	English Translation
Kuuipo	*Sweetheart*
Puuwai	*Love, affection*
Aloha au ia 'oe	*I love you*
Aloha wui loa	*Very much love*
Malama	*To take care of, fidelity*
Makana	*Gift, present*
Ko maua la male 'ana	*Our wedding day*
Male 'ana	*Wedding*
Kuaua	*Shower*
Ho 'olau le 'a	*Celebration*
Mau loa	*Forever*
Ke aloha	*Beloved*
Nau ko 'u aloha	*My love is yours*
Nou no ka 'tini	*I desire you*
Ka 'u la e lei a 'e nei la	*I pledge my love to you alone*
Honi	*Kiss*
Wahine Male	*Married woman*
Male	*Married man*
Ho 'oku 'I	*To join together*
Hau 'oli	*Happy*

photo mat keepsake

Help the bride- and groom-to-be remember their luau shower with a framed picture. Before the shower, purchase a ready-made photo mat. Have guests sign the mat, then use it as the mat for a photo of the couple taken at the luau. Look for a ready-made frame with an island style to house the mat and photo.

Favor Ideas

In addition to the leis your guests will receive as they arrive, present each of the women with an ornamental flower. Ask each to place the flower behind her ear, placing it behind the left ear (closest to her heart) if she is in a relationship or behind the right if she is single and available.

Invitation Flowers on page 88, Lei Flowers on page 92 and Banner Flowers on page 88 *Invitation flowers appear here at full size. For the name tag lei on page 92, enlarge pattern at 147%. For the banner flower on page 88, enlarge at 200%, again at 200%, then at 106% to bring to full size*

resources

All of the materials used in the projects in this book can be purchased at your local craft, fabric, scrapbooking and rubber stamping stores or at discount department stores. If you are unable to find what you need at a local store, contact the manufacturers listed below for a retailer near you.

Decorative Papers

KI Memories
(972) 243-5595
Fax: (972) 712-1164
www.kimemories.com
"Fire Barcode" paper
"Fire Dot" paper
"Hazard Linen" paper

Paper Source
(312) 906-9678
www.paper-source.com

Paper Style
11390 Old Roswell Rd.
Suite 122
Alpharetta, GA 30004
(800) 670-5300
www.paperstyle.com
Anna Griffin papers, ribbon

Papercrafting Supplies

Hero Arts
www.heroarts.com
Letter stamps

Kolo, LLC.
P.O. Box 572
Windsor, CT 06095
(888) 636-5656
www.kolo.com
Mini album

Making Memories
1168 West 500 North
Centerville, UT 84014
(801) 294-0430
www.makingmemories.com
Lavender ribbon
Metal eyelets
Wedding word washers

**Plaid Enterprises, Inc.
(All Night Media)**
3225 Westech Drive
Norcross, GA 30092
(800) 842-4197
www.plaidonline.com
"Something Borrowed..." stamp
FolkArt paints
Cardboard gift bags
Brass Seasons Stencil
Stamp Art Gift Box

Scrapbook.com
116 N. Lindsay Rd. #3
Mesa, AZ 85213
(800) 727-2726
www.scrapbook.com
SEI Papers
Page pebbles

Scrapbook Express
www.scrapbookexpress.com

Containers and Boxes

**Alpine Dynamics
(Best Containers)**
10939 N. Alpine Hwy.
Suite 510
Highland, UT 84003
(925) 209-8000
Fax: (801) 705-1644
www.bestcontainers.com
Paint cans, large and small

Walnut Hollow Farm, Inc.
1409 State Road 23
Dodgeville, WI 53533
(800) 950-5101
www.walnuthollow.com
Recipe box

Food and Drink

Jelly Belly Candy Company
One Jelly Belly Lane
Fairfield, CA 94533
(800) 522-3267
www.jellybelly.com
Candy pieces in a wide assortment of colors

Jones Soda
Jones Soda Seattle
234 9th Avenue North
Seattle, WA 98109
(800) 656-6050
Fax: (206) 624-6857
www.jonessoda.com
Brightly colored sodas

M&M/Mars
www.mms.com
Candy pieces in a wide assortment of colors

Other Resources

Two Peas in a Bucket
www.twopeasinabucket.com
Fonts

index

A

Adhesives, 9

B

Bone folder, 8

C

Cardstock, 8
Craft glue, 9
Craft knife, 8
Cutting mat, 8

D

Decoration projects
    Bride and Groom Name
        Banner, 16
    Hanging Clothesline, 65
    Love Banner, 82
    Love in Paradise Sign, 90
    Luminary, 32-34
    Napkin Rings, 31
    Take-out Lunch, 16
    Wheat Grass Paint Can, 13
Découpage medium, 9

E

Entertainment. See Games
    and Entertainment
Eyelets, setting, 11

F

Favors
    Candy Tin Favor, 19
    Heart Candles Favor, 84
    Lavender Soap Favor, 52
    Mini Laundry Bag
        Favor, 66-67
    Muffin Mix Favor, 42
    Napkin Rings Favor, 74-75
    Tussie-Mussie Favor, 60
Food. See Recipes

G

Games and Entertainment
    Avocado Facial Mask, 51
    Banana Facial Mask, 51
    Build-A-Story Game, 18
    Foot and Hand Scrub, 51
    Guess the Spice Game, 43
    Hawaiian Word Game, 92
    "How Well Do You Know
        Me?" Game, 24
    Kitchen Utensil Game, 43

Language of Flowers
        Game, 59
    Laundry Basket Game, 66
    Love on the Line Game, 66
    Marriage Memory Game, 18
    Movie and Song Matching
        Game, 82
    Photo Match Game, 76
    Ribbon Charm Pull
        Game, 59
    Thirteen Coins Game, 36
    Water Balloon Volleyball
        Game, 24
    Wedding Word Blackout
        Game, 51
Gift Projects. See also Favors,
    Keepsakes
    Towel Cake Gift, 69
Grommets, setting, 11

I

Invitations
    Bath Salts Invitation, 48-49
    Clothesline Invitation, 64
    Fiesta Heart Invitation, 30
    Hawaiian Invitation, 88-89
    Kitchen Apron Invitation,
        40-41
    Lingerie Bag Invitation,
        80-81
    Seasons Invitation, 72-73
    Time of Day Invitation,
        14-15
    Victorian Charm Invitation,
        56-57
    Water Bubbles Invitation,
        22-23

K

Keepsakes
    Album Keepsake, 53
    Candy Tin Favor, 19
    Coaster Keepsake, 26-27
    Mini Photo Album
        Keepsake, 37
    Photo Mat Keepsake, 93
    Recipe Box Keepsake, 43-45
    Romantic Advice
        Keepsake, 85
    Serving Tray Keepsake, 61
    Wedding Wreath
        Keepsake, 74

M

Materials
    adhesives, 9
    bone folder, 8
    cardstock, 8
    craft glue, 9
    craft knife, 8
    cutting mat, 8
    découpage medium, 9
    embellishments, 9
    glue stick, 9
    hot glue, 9
    paper, 8
    ruler, 8
    scissors, 8
    spray adhesive, 9
    stylus, 8
    text paper, 8
    translucent paper, 8

P

Paper
    cardstock, 8
    text paper, 8
    translucent paper, 8
Punching holes, 10

R

Recipes
    Berry Smoothies, 50
    Better-Than-Sex Cake, 25
    Broccoli Cheese Salad, 17
    Chicken and Sausage
        Shish Kabobs, 25
    Chicken Salad, 77
    Chocolate Fondue, 83
    Fajitas, 35
    Frothy Ocean Cooler, 25
    Fruit Dip, 68
    Giant Gingersnaps, 17
    Hash Browned Potatoes, 58
    Honey Butter, 41
    Honeymoon "Passion"
        Punch, 91
    Hummus Dip, 50
    Laurie's Raspberry
        Lemonade, 41
    Lemon Daffodil Cake, 58
    Love Fortune Cookies, 83
    Mild Salsa, 35
    No-Bake Lemon
        Cheesecake, 68
    Oven Roasted Pork, 91

    Pita Wedges, 50
    Sparkling Cranberry
        Punch, 83
Resources, 94
Ruler, 8

S

Scissors, 8
Scoring paper, 10
Spray adhesive, 9
Stylus, 8
Suppliers, 9

T

Techniques
    eyelets, setting, 11
    grommets, setting, 11
    punching holes, 10
    scoring and folding
        paper, 10
Themes
    To Everything a Season,
        70-77
    Fiesta, Mi Amor, 28-37
    Fresh Laundry, 62-69
    Love is in the Air, 78-85
    Luxury Bridal Spa, 46-53
    Paradise Luau, 86-93
    Something Borrowed,
        Something Blue, 54-61
    Taking the Plunge, 20-27
    What Time Is It?, 12-19

The best in wedding inspirations and creative crafts comes from North Light Books!

New Inspirations in Wedding Florals

You can create beautiful wedding florals that look professionally crafted with the guidance of Terry Rye. Whether you're an experienced flower arranger or a beginner, *New Inspirations in Wedding Florals* provides expert tips and techniques to make your wedding even lovelier. Included are 30 unique, step-by-step projects with variations such as bridal and bridesmaid bouquets, arrangements for the ceremony, table centerpieces, cake toppers and more!

ISBN 1-55870-634-8, paperback, 128 pages, #70582-K

Greeting Cards for Every Occasion

Renowned crafter MaryJo McGraw shares her most creative card ideas. With complete, step-by-step instructions and 23 detailed projects, it's easy to make your sentiments more personal and meaningful. You'll find a wealth of inspiring card ideas for nearly every holiday and occasion, including Christmas, Valentine's Day, Mother's and Father's Day, birthday, get well soon, new job and much more!

ISBN 1-58180-410-5, paperback, 128 pages, #32580-K

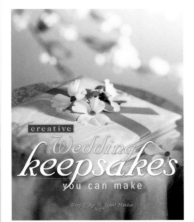

Creative Wedding Keepsakes

Make your wedding elegant and unforgettable with these beautiful keepsake ideas. From the bridal veil to the guest book, this book provides 21 step-by-step projects that are fun, affordable and surprisingly easy to make. Best of all, each project is made from non-perishable materials, so everything can be finished well in advance of the big day.

ISBN 1-55870-559-7, paperback, 128 pages, #70487-K

Beautiful Bridal Accessories You Can Make

Here's a smart, sophisticated alternative to store-bought wedding accessories. Jackie Johnson shows you how to make an incredible variety of elegant adornments for the bride, wedding party, friends and family. Personalized to fit your style, each of these 22 step-by-step projects is inexpensive and easy-to-make with simple embellishing techniques and a glue gun.

ISBN 1-55870-624-0, paperback, 128 pages, #70570-K

Wedding Papercrafts

Make your wedding a unique and memorable event full of your own personal style. Inside this book are over 50 personalized projects to make your wedding one-of-a-kind. Easy-to-follow instructions guide you every step of the way in creating professional-looking projects. Whether you're a beginner or an experienced papercrafter, you'll find valuable guidance and inspiration including 10 unique themes showcasing invitations and coordinated projects such as guest books.

ISBN 1-55870-653-4, paperback, 128 pages, #70603-K

These and other fine North Light titles are available from your local art & craft retailer, bookstore, online supplier or by calling 1-800-448-0915.

North Light Books

96